The Sunnyside of Heartache

Brenda Murphy

Scripture quotations marked ESV are from The ESV® Bible (The Holy Bible, English Standard Version®), © 2001 by Crossway, a publishing ministry of Good News Publishers. Used by permission. All rights reserved.

Scripture quotations marked KJV are from The Authorized (King James) Version. Rights in the Authorized Version in the United Kingdom are vested in the Crown. Reproduced by permission of the Crown's patentee, Cambridge University Press

Scripture quotations marked NASB are taken from the (NASB®) New American Standard Bible®, Copyright © 1960, 1971, 1977, 1995, 2020 by The Lockman Foundation. Used by permission. All rights reserved. www.Lockman.org

Scripture quotations marked NIV are taken from The Holy Bible, New International Version® NIV® Copyright © 1973, 1978, 1984, 2011 by Biblica, Inc. Used with permission. All rights reserved worldwide.

Scripture quotations marked (NLT) are taken from the Holy Bible, New Living Translation, copyright ©1996, 2004, 2015 by Tyndale House Foundation. Used by permission of Tyndale House Publishers, Carol Stream, Illinois 60188. All rights reserved.

Cover Design by Rick Schroeppel
https://www.bookcoverdesign.us/

Interior Design by Lisa Bell
https://www.bylisabell.com

Copyright © 2026 by Brenda Murphy

All rights reserved.

No portion of this book may be reproduced in any form without written permission from the publisher or author, except as permitted by U.S. copyright law.

Paperback ISBN: 978-1-965561-18-8
Ebook ISBN: 978-1-965561-19-5

In memory of Audie Murphy, my beloved husband and partner in this journey of life for more than 38 years.

Contents

Acknowledgment	IX
The Sunnyside of Heartache	
Contents	2
Forewords	4
Preface	6
1. The Place of Heartache	7
2. Rain, Rain Please Go Away	21
3. Self-Care is Vital	29
4. Considerate of Others' Pain	39
5. Take Your Time	47
6. Everything Matters	53
7. New Boundaries for the Journey Ahead	59
8. It's so Hard to say Goodbye to Yesterday	65
9. Nurturing Your Garden	73
10. Spiritual Eyes Wide Open	81
11. God's Got a Blessing With my Name on It	87

12.	Trusting God With Your Future	91
13.	When God Whispers Your Name	99
14.	The Next Chapter	107
15.	It Gets Greater Later	115
16.	Strategic Planning	119
17.	Setting the Stage for Success	123
18.	The Lifter of my Head	129
19.	From Restricted to Being Reserved	139
20.	Resting in Wait	153
21.	The Tour Guide Knows the Route	159

References	179
About the Author	181
Also by	183

The Sunnyside of Heartache
Companion Activities for Personal Growth and Healing

Contents		186
Fullpage image		188
1.	The Sunnyside of Heartache Workbook	189
2.	How to Use This Workbook	191
3.	Section One: Acknowledging Heartache	192
4.	Section Two: Finding the Sunnyside of Your Personal Heartache	194

5.	Section Three: Moving Forward Through Your Private Pain	196
6.	Section Four: The Importance of Self-Care in Your Heartache	198
7.	Section Five: Making Your Personal a Priority in Your Healing	200
8.	Section Six: Setting New Boundaries for the Journey Ahead	202
9.	Section Seven: Having a New Perspective in The Journey Ahead:	204
10.	Section Eight: Trusting God With Your Future	206
11.	Section Nine: Finding Rest in God While Processing Your Personal Pain	208
12.	Section Ten: Trusting God With Your Future:	210
13.	Section Eleven: It Greater Later:	212
14.	Section Twelve: How Important is it to be Patient With Your New Chapter?	214
15.	Section Thirteen: Finding Rest in God While Processing Personal Pain	216
16.	Section Fourteen: Setting The Stage For Future Success	218
17.	Conclusion	220
18.	Embracing God's Timing for Your Life	224

19. Notes & Reflections	226
20. Closing Thoughts	232
21. Closing Prayer for Healing from Heartache	243
About the author	245
Also by Brenda Murphy	247

Acknowledgment

This book is dedicated to a life well lived together with my amazing, God-fearing husband and covering, Audie Murphy. Together, we shared an incredible life filled with joy, hardship, and pain. Through it all, we learned how to weather all the storms with guidance, faith, belief, and happiness, plus peace and respect for one another.

Throughout our lifetime, we spent quality time learning how to stick together, pray together, believe together, and trust God together. We were both rewarded through the much-needed grace and mercy of God, gelling us together.

Over the past 38 years, Audie and I personally watched our God take our heartache and pain and grow it into a greater form of love, appreciation, respect, and adoration for one another.

Audie, even though our time well spent on earth is no more, I am still forever grateful to God for giving me a covering that loved and cherished what we both shared.

I will forever value and treasure the life lessons I learned through you, such as love deeply, laugh often, and always live a life of total gratitude for everything good in my life!

Thank you, sweetheart, and I will see you one day on the other Sunny Side of my Heartache!

Brenda

The Sunny Side of Heartache

Psalms 118:8 (KJV)

"It is better to trust in the LORD than to put confidence in man."

I called upon the LORD in distress: the LORD answered me and set me in a large place. The LORD is on my side; I will not fear: what can man do unto me? The LORD taketh my part with them that help me: therefore, shall I see my desire upon them that hate me. **It is better to trust in the LORD than to put confidence in man.** *It is better to trust in the LORD than to put confidence in princes. All nations compassed me about: but in the name of the LORD will I destroy them. They compassed me about; yea, they compassed me about: but in the name of the LORD, I will destroy them.*

Psalm 118:5-12 (KJV)

The Sunnyside of Heartache

Brenda Murphy

Contents

Forewords	4
Preface	6
1. The Place of Heartache	7
2. Rain, Rain Please Go Away	21
3. Self-Care is Vital	29
4. Considerate of Others' Pain	39
5. Take Your Time	47
6. Everything Matters	53
7. New Boundaries for the Journey Ahead	59
8. It's so Hard to say Goodbye to Yesterday	65
9. Nurturing Your Garden	73
10. Spiritual Eyes Wide Open	81
11. God's Got a Blessing With my Name on It	87
12. Trusting God With Your Future	91
13. When God Whispers Your Name	99
14. The Next Chapter	107

15. It Gets Greater Later	115
16. Strategic Planning	119
17. Setting the Stage for Success	123
18. The Lifter of my Head	129
19. From Restricted to Being Reserved	139
20. Resting in Wait	153
21. The Tour Guide Knows the Route	159
References	179
About the Author	181
Also by	183

Forewords

I have known Minister Brenda for a few years. She is a woman of God.

I have read most of her books. She loves God, and she loves God's people. She is not a game player. She is a life changer, a teacher, and a minister who enjoys administering God's Word.

Through her Tribe Ministry class, Minister Brenda teaches our class how to pursue God and to live following Christ every day. What I have personally learned through Minister Brenda's teaching is how to build my life on a solid foundation through reading and believing the Word of God.

Through her teaching, I am learning how to hold on to God, have a deeper desire to know Him personally, and strive to become more like Jesus. Minister Murphy is a God-fearing woman. I have seen in her good times as well as some of her most difficult times, and in both, she has never ceased to trust God.

While I am not sure what this book, *The Sunny Side of Heartache* will be about, I have every confidence it will be a good read like all her other books. It will be a blessing and will inspire others as well.

Minister Brenda, I believe your book will inspire and foster encouragement to family, friends, and the world, because you possess the zeal to inspire others in your audience to build their lives in Jesus Christ through faith and prayer.

Jean Coward

Life isn't always what we plan it to be, but some take what is and use it to become what God created it to be. The author of this latest book, *The Sunnyside of Heartache*, has been on a faith walk with God to become all that God has created her to be. I have personally witnessed Brenda Murphy's faith walk as she planned her very first conference to her increased speaking engagements and her teachings. She demonstrates unshakable faith in her daily walk.

Her books contain many of her personal experiences that countless people can relate to. Her faith in God has enabled her to forge ahead in penning books that share experiences such as lost, gains, disappointments, betrayal, expected support and successes—things many can relate to.

I look forward to the gem that will be discovered in this book which will increase the faith walk of the believer and enable one to overcome those barriers that are unknown in one's life.

I encourage you to sit back and discover the jewel that awaits you while you join this faith walk and read Brenda Murphy's latest book *The Sunnyside of Heartache*.

Earline Franklin
Life Group Teacher
Former BSF Discussion Leader

Preface

It's hard to depend on God when we are used to relying on ourselves. But the Bible teaches how to build confidence in God, not self.

As I look back into some of the earlier years of my life, I can faintly remember some specific times in the earlier years of my childhood when I felt insecure about how I looked, talked, and performed in school and eventually in my career and life in general. I was afraid of rejection or not being liked in friendships and in the view of others.

Little did I realize I was giving too much of my strength, life, and myself over to others to decide for me what I should do, how I should do it, and yes, eventually, if I should do it. Now that I know better, I shudder to think about how far down the road I could have been or even should have been.

What I know now that I did not realize before—never ask others to define you through their imaginations. For one, their lenses will always be too small to cover all the intricate details of how God made you and His intended purpose for your life. That is a job only the True and Living God can do and should be allowed to do. For the record, never give up that sacred place for anyone or anything.

Always look to God, the Author and the Finisher of your soul. Allow His voice to have full reign in your life and in the image that you see in the mirror. Immediately agree with God that you are exactly who He declared you and your life to be and never exchange who you are for doubt and speculation—no matter the cost.

Chapter One

The Place of Heartache

JUST THE MENTION OF the word "heartache" is a place where I would like nothing more than to avoid all the days of my natural life. It can be a place of uncomfortableness and deep discomfort. A place where it seems nothing good can or ever will come from it. A place that sets the tone for loneliness, hurt, old wounds to flare up, and filled with nothing left but bitterness and utter regret.

At the outset, heartache can be a place of confusion and, at times, disillusion; at other times pure numbness and even denial. One minute you are sure about your direction, and the next, you are not clear at all. Sometimes you want to move forward, and at other times, you feel stuck in the midst of it all without the proper strength or desire to move forward.

Heartache is just that—heartache. It is a heart that has been wounded, damaged, broken, and undivided by life's circumstances and events. At times, heartache can appear to be the epitome of brokenness. Your heart is at the center of attraction.

When heartache happens to you, in that moment, it is easy to feel as though you will never be put back together again. Your whole world appears shattered into a thousand pieces, and there is not enough superglue in the world that could put it back together again. You may feel like you have been robbed of your true joy, peace, laughter, and even love. And it isn't fair.

Heartache is a pain that can devastate your whole world as you once knew it. It can leave you stripped of all your previous confidence and assuredness. And heartache can happen at any moment without the slightest hint of warning and catch you without warning. Pain can literally knock you off your feet and totally blindside you in a moment's notice. If you don't make conscious decisions about your life, it can render you disabled for the rest of your life.

It does not matter how prepared we think we may be. Heartache is a dream killer with a silencer on the end of the smoking gun. No matter how well trained and poised you may think or believe you are ready to deal with heartache, by the time it finishes with you, it may leave you questioning your entire existence and what your real purpose may have been.

Heartache is not only a dream killer but a grave robber. It is intense, fresh, relentless, and intentional. Heartache is not a friend to anyone at any time. However, the one thing I can say about heartache is that it takes no prisoners, and it does not discriminate.

Heartache does not care about you, your parents' names, your pedigree, your financial portfolio, your college degrees, your status quo. At some point, heartache comes for all and makes no apologies in its aftermath.

Heartache creeps up on you. It doesn't just happen overnight. If we look carefully, there are times when heartache leaves us little clues and cues about how it entered our lives, because we are not looking out for it. We are just going about our daily tasks, and before you know, it shows up undetected. Sometimes, it remains for a long time.

Take, for instance, that you noticed for several days you had "this feeling" in the pit of your stomach that something not so good was going to happen. But you could not put your finger on it. However, the feeling gnawing at you lingered. No matter what, you could not let it go for the life of you. Every time you tried to put it out of your mind, you could not shake it.

Finally, the day came, and so did the thing you feared the most.

The phone call came. "I am calling to inform you that your son or daughter was in a car accident and didn't make it."

Heartache at its finest.

You get to work, and your supervisor or boss wants to meet with you first thing in their office. "Last hired, first fired due to budget cuts. Sorry, we have to let you go."

Heartache at its finest with no place to go.

Heartache can swoop in and completely change the total trajectory of your life, almost making you want to completely throw in the towel and walk away from it all—the good, the bad, and the ugly.

They say heartache comes to make you strong, and on some level in life it does. However, there are other times when you feel totally the opposite.

When heartache arrives, it can be so subtle it knocks the very breath out of your lungs. You cannot breathe, you become dizzy, and you cannot even speak. When you do, the words are not always audible or make any sense.

When personal heartache places you directly in the line of fire, you no longer feel your feet on the ground. For a moment, you may think it is a prank of some sort. A horrible joke being played on you with a punch line sooner than later.

For beginners, heartache sends your heart and emotions through a roller-coaster ride like you have never been on before. At first, you are clueless and question whether what you just experienced is absolutely true or if you are in some type of fog or illusion.

You tell yourself, "No this cannot be true. It cannot be happening." What did you do to deserve this pain, this loss, this regret, this embarrassment, this misunderstanding, or this hurt? Heartache makes you feel empty, incomplete, misunderstood, and disappointed.

I have come to understand personally that without the help of God at the forefront of my life, I am sure I would be unable to move forward. I would not be able to weather this current storm in my life. Alone. I am not 100% sure if I would even want to.

Hurt is a lot of things, but one particular thing hurt isn't is consistent. It is not identical. Hurt is not a twin or akin to any other pain. It truly stands alone. It is different and feels different for each of us. There is no cookie cutter for heartache. It is indeed in a class all by itself.

People try their best to encourage you, coach you, check on you, and even pray for you. However, at that specific moment, your pain is almost always screaming louder than the conversation you desperately try to wrap your mind around.

Hurt tugs at your heartstrings and emotions because it wants nothing less than to render you useless to yourself and those around you. One of its sole desires is to strip you of any chance to bounce back from overwhelming pain and despair.

Intense pain can cause one to question every single thing about their new environment.

Everything you once were 100% assured about is now called into question. You wonder to yourself whether you can continue to move forward or even whether you should. You start to look around at the shattered pieces that remain, and you ponder whether it is worth the effort of trying to start all over again.

There is so much new to do. There are so many necessary things you have to change and look at differently. There is no real rush to change overnight. It is going to take time for you to heal and let the hurt go slowly but assuredly.

When heartache strikes, it does not provide you with a forewarning. It does not introduce itself as a robber of sorts, nor does it need an invitation to invade your life of true love, pure joy, or your genuine peace. It simply interrupts your life no matter what stage or interval your life may be in. Heartache can leave you filled with immeasurable regret and possible unexplainable rage.

Heartache can be harsh. Deliberate. Raw. Brutal and intentional. At other times, heartache can be demanding and determined, especially when you don't see it coming. It can crush your heart into bits and pieces and dash all your dreams, rendering you dead inside even when you smile on the outside.

Heartache can, and often does, affect every part of your everyday life. It starts with the mind and works all the way down through your emotions. At first, you think your mind is playing tricks on you. You are not 100% sure anymore if what you thought you went through is accurate or a dream.

You make every effort to try and make sense of what no longer makes sense. When all the pieces do not fit together like you once remembered, your mind sends clouds of doubt, laced with uncertainties and confusion, that can be followed by fear of the unknown.

Heartache is a diverse language that speaks to everyone differently and through various formats. How one individual handles heartache is on a totally different platform than someone else. One of the main things to remember when heartache knocks at your door is that the pain you feel right now is private and personal and debilitating. It will take you immeasurable time to even think about the healing process. It is going to take a respectable amount of time to tunnel through.

Some people perform their best work or deal with heartache as an opportunity to soar higher above adversity and allow their personal pain to thrust them into another dimension of themselves they never knew existed. Again, this will take time and is a process to accomplish. Everyone is different, and the process should never be seen as a competition.

While we can ascertain that with proper time, one can move beyond the pain and heartache of our heartbreaks. There is no specific timeframe for doing so. And if anyone questions the timing of your pain, they are absolutely and completely out of line. Your timeframe for the threshold of your pain is both private and personal. Quite frankly, it is no one else's business but yours.

Because of the world's obsessiveness about moving on to the next thing, no matter what that might be, trying to rush your emotions and your true feelings can prove unhealthy and unreasonable. If the right measures are not taken seriously, there is a strong possibility of reverting to more pain.

Sadly, there are others who view heartache as a death sentence and not a stepping stone, because they cannot see any possible way of moving forward without looking back or living their lives full of regret and unresolved issues.

For them, the fight to keep their sanity, the loneliness that challenges their "new normal," the fresh wounds that come about as a result of their new journey can be too much to undertake at one time. It can become overwhelming to say the least.

Heartache can challenge even the best of us. It is not about being stronger than others or being the weakest link in the chain. It is all about thriving while being held semi-hostage in survival mode, looking forward to brighter days ahead.

When you are heartbroken, it is possible to see brighter days ahead. But from your vantage point, the distance to get back on the road to recovery again seems insurmountable and at times, humanly impossible.

For a person in survival mode to get back to themselves where they can laugh again, relax, and become their renewed selves, it doesn't come without a genuine fight, desire, and will to move forward. After all, you have to start from scratch without a blueprint to provide guidance.

There should never be a question about whether an individual wants to feel alive again, because he or she does. They desperately want to feel alive and happy again, but the process has no quick shortcuts to getting there. You have to take the appropriate time to get there without explanation or questioning.

During these moments, it is absolutely vital to have your tribe around you—those who cover you in prayer and shield you in compassion and wisdom while you are rendered too weak or overwhelmed to move forward on your own.

It is imperative to have and to know your village. If you do not have the correct village around you, the people who circle you can actually create more havoc than peace and therefore cause greater disturbance rather than benefit your next chapter in life.

My most severe level of heartache came not when my beloved spouse passed away but actually sixteen and a half years ago when

I came home and found him having a massive stroke in our home office. I remember it vividly. That day, my whole life as I knew it shifted.

In September 2012, our lives, as we knew them, changed forever in a single day. Heartache for both of our lives invaded us and reeked various levels of unexplainable pain beyond what one could possibly imagine and then some.

After a while, I realized that if there was any possible chance of survival for both me and my spouse, I needed to rest in God—not sometimes but completely. As the days proceeded into countless years, I learned authentically what it meant to sing and know what an authentic friend I had in Jesus.

The name of the Lord became my high place and my supernatural high tower—my personal place of refuge and my authentic strength. I found God to be a refuge behind the wall at which I often found my back up against. In the midst of it all, Jesus became my forever stay.

During the most horrendous times, Jesus alone was my Comforter, Friend, Confidante, my Helper and my Lord. Even though I became acquainted with Him at the age of nine, I chased after Him ever since. The more I got to know Him, the more I wanted to intimately know about Him.

In 2012, the courtship of our everyday living in Christ became increasingly intense for me and my spouse. Little did I know the days and weeks would soon translate into months and years—16 ½ to be exact.

Just when I thought I would break and lose it, I heard in the Holy Spirit that the Lord was calling me to follow Him into the deeper parts of the unknown by faith and belief.

I know now what I would not have understood without heartache. So many levels in our walk with Christ can only grow through heartache and pain and by relinquishing all of ourselves into the hands of an all-knowing and all-seeing capable God.

I now know it is not necessary to understand to my satisfaction all the events taking place in my life. Rather, I must trust the One who orchestrated the events from the beginning to the end. I am learning on my new journey to stop trying to make my life make sense and merely trust the One who has always walked beside me in the unknown.

I have to trust, relinquish, and choose to believe the plans He has for me are far greater and more pleasurable than I can dream or imagine, not forgetting it is all in God's great timing.

I always say and believe that God never makes sense, but He will always make wisdom. Therefore, now in my life, I strive to get wisdom because I know for myself the wisdom of God is my principal desire. Over the years, through my personal experience even while feeling some days like the assignment was too much and too heavy, I knew in my heart of hearts that God was with me.

Over the years of tunneling through, I learned how to really trust, lean, and depend upon Jesus. I found Him to be closer than I ever imagined. I didn't have to pray loudly; I could whisper His name, and He was there. He is my faithful friend, a dependable confidant, and a caring God.

There are some who believe they are the most blessed when they are on top of the mountain and avoiding the valley at all costs. But I have found the mountaintop is fleeting, and the valley is sustainable—especially when you realize and recognize God to be the Good Shepherd that leads you beside the still waters.

No matter which location or place you find yourself currently in, we serve a God who covers both bases well. He will never leave you or ever forsake you. He is very true to His Word, because He alone is His own Word.

It really is so sweet when I trust in Jesus. I close my eyes and bask in His presence. I take comfort in resting in Him. I've learned how to take Him at His Word. After all, He has proven Himself to me over and over again.

Through those early years of Audie's and my journey, we both witnessed and experienced the goodness of God in real time. We've seen the great arm of God resting over our lives together as well as apart.

We have experienced God's personal glory ministering and even administering to us, especially in the worst of times.

Together, we watched Him bring us out grander and greater than we went into the warfare or the fire. We saw God open doors no man could shut. We saw God show up in the hospital at Audie's bedside and heal his body when the doctors informed me there was blood on his brain and that Audie possibly might not make it through the night. I saw God provide a strong yes when the doctors and nurses for sure thought it would be a unanimous hard no.

There is no one like Jesus! No one remotely close to Him can keep you like Jesus can. He alone was and is my stay. In my personal heartache, I discovered Him to be my Comforter and my Comforting King.

Even though the separation from the love of my earthly life is painful and challenging at times, I know I am not alone or without hope, because I feel the arms of God all around me. And I feel the love of my incredible covering in my heart every day. I know beyond a shadow of a doubt that I am loved by both, and it warms my heart to unspecified limits.

As I continue to relinquish my pain and sorrow over the separation of my beautiful life with my incredible covering in the natural, I am so thankful to God for the 38 beautiful years we shared together.

They were like an incredible fairytale that could only have been written by God. Our times shared together are forever etched in my heart. Our journey together wasn't always flawless, but it was ordained by the Lord. We sojourned together through them until the day of his passing and going home to be with the Lord forever.

I remember vividly the first year of our marriage.

The Holy Spirit spoke to my heart and said, "Brenda, you do not know how to be a wife, and Audie doesn't know how to be a husband. But if you allow me, I will put myself in the middle and keep you both."

And that is exactly what God did for us.

Finally, I would like to say this. Don't worry and fret about heartache, because it is a part of life. There is no way around it. In fact, embrace it wholeheartedly and go into it with your shattered heart, tear-stained eyes, broken dreams, frustrations, anger, doubts, and pain. Then watch God turn it around for your good and His glory!

Don't get in a corner and shrivel up. Don't put your head in the sand and declare that life is over. Don't let anyone tell you your life isn't worth living just because your heart has been broken, or you have been left for dead by your circumstances. Remember God is always able.

Decree and declare over your life that these ashes are temporary. This heartache is not going to be the end of your story but the ingredients for something new—necessary and vital for your next chapter and godly assignment.

Run, don't walk, and purposely choose to lay down at the feet of Jesus and allow His favor to be poured all over your mind, heart, and soul. Look to Him for direction, guidance, leadership, purpose, and favor.

Allow Jesus to make you new. Ask Him to fortify you from the inside out. To provide you with a fresh wind that will propel you higher than you have ever been before.

Grieve what you must grieve and take personal ownership of your tears and heartache, because every tear has its own language. Even though others will not always understand your hurt, wounds, and sorrow, they don't have to, because it is your pain.

Take it all to Jesus and let Him unscramble the eggs of pain in your journey. Just remember He that began a good work in your personal journey is the same Tour Guide that is going to continue to guide you through it all.

I say celebrate the good, the bad, the intentional, the faults, and the failures, because every experience we personally encounter comes to teach us vital things about ourselves. They can make us stronger if we have the capacity to allow them to.

Be mindful of who is providing you with unsolicited advice especially when what you are going through is not their personal testimony. Stay close to God and allow Him to direct your steps, because when you follow others' suggestions, it is inevitable that the directions through their lens can most often become misconstrued.

Days after burying my beloved sweetheart, I am learning how to navigate through the waves of feelings and new emotions that come with heartache. I am accepting the fact that no matter how much others love me, they cannot take this very private journey with me. I must go on it alone.

But I am not alone. Jesus is constantly by my side, and for that, I am very grateful. Daily, I am accepting God's love for me from a different perspective. Instead of looking at my new life, new chapter as being a loss or abandonment, I have come into agreement with God that His plans He has for me are greater than I could possibly plan for myself.

While each day since the burial of my husband is still fresh and very much real, I am also gaining greater insight. The loss of my husband from my physical life does not have to mean the end of all my special and wonderful memories we created together.

It just means there is a brand-new chapter now being written in my life, and if I am open to it, it can become a sweet new dawning that awaits me.

I know God loves me more than I can fathom. I know His love for me is genuine and pure. I know that despite my current pain, underneath it all are the wings of a loving, caring, and Almighty God carrying me through it all.

I am surrounded by beautiful, saved, and anointed family and friends who are praying for me constantly and honestly wanting the very best for me. Daily, they make their intentions known to me and serve with gladness. God is truly good to me.

Awareness of God posting beautiful angels from every direction to come to my side when I need it most makes me smile both inside and out. It simply reminds me that God is mindful of me.

It puts me in the mind of the scripture that reads in Isaiah 52:7 (NIV), "How beautiful on the mountains are the feet of those who bring good news, who proclaim peace, who bring good tidings, who proclaim salvation, who say to Zion, 'Your God reigns!'"

The wonderful circle of friends that came to help me in my truest time of need were undoubtedly sent by God. No less than to assist me in my overall healing and to make sure I received the necessary rest when I needed it most.

For that, I am beyond thankful and blessed. Their presence in my life continues to provide a sense of assurance that life continues even when heartache invades your privacy. Through their genuine love and comforting words, I feel my strength growing day by day.

I believe that accepting heartache when it is raw and fresh can be a blessing in itself. By embracing heartache head-on without any strings of expectation or explanation allows God to show Himself stronger in my life.

This was another opportunity for me to see God in my life at His finest. I am learning that at this juncture in my life, I do not have to say a lot, but rather simply to rest and trust Him and His plans for my future.

Over the years of my walk with Christ, I have experienced God's love for me on many levels, and now is another opportunity to see Him from another level.

While I am nervous on some level about the next chapter in my life, I must say I am intrigued to see what lies ahead for me and the journey clearly unfolding right before my very eyes.

I can be excited, because I trust the One who has written the chapters that lie ahead. He knows my heart and my intentions, which have always been to do His express will of ministering to His children.

I enjoy making an impact in the lives of others. I love it when people, including myself, are hungry for the Word of God and cannot wait to draw closer to Him. I love sharing the gospel with literally everyone I come into contact with and watching their eyes light up.

I live to love God with my whole heart. He has done so much for me and has changed me immensely, and for that, I am humbly thankful and appreciative.

I cannot praise Him enough. I cannot thank Him enough. And the only way I continue to show my gratitude to Him is to serve Him in a way I was created to do—that is to let my little light shine on the earth.

There is a phrase that goes something like this. "He's done so much for me, that I cannot tell it all!" That is my sentiment exactly. The love of God provides so much unspeakable joy and excitement for me that I cannot ever tell it all.

For as long as I can remember, I lived, thought, breathed ministry ever since I was a little girl. Not just the name "ministry," but the service of what ministry is. I live to talk about my Savior. I love His name and His will in and over my life.

Over the years, He changed me from the inside out. Even today, He is still working on me and continuously making me over in ways I could have never imagined. I am honestly in awe of it all.

I will forever be thankful for what God does in my life. I am grateful I am not the same person that I started my life's journey with at the age of nine. I do not have the room or the time to testify of God's goodness in my life or the miracles He has done. However, what I do know is that I am forever thankful.

God is a mighty good healer and an incredible Leader. If I had to describe my life journey as it relates to Christ being at the helm, I would have to say a walking miracle time and time again. It is only through Him that I live today and have my perfect being.

Yes, heartache is a tough pill to swallow or to wrap our hearts around. No one likes the taste of heartache on any level and would do almost anything to avoid it. Unfortunately, that is a subject matter that cannot be denied. No matter the talent, ability or skill, or the pedigree in life, heartache comes to all. At times, it may appear to stay for a while without the possibility of eviction. It is inevitable for everyone at some point in life. However, embracing heartache can be adventurous and challenging at the same time.

If embraced, heartache can show you what's genuine in your heart, what's pure in your mind, and also what's not. It can also show you how much you depend upon God, or don't, and what areas in your life have room for improvement and acceptance.

During Audie's and my sixteen and a half years of caregiving together, we experienced God's arm resting over our lives. Together, we literally saw God's faithfulness up close and personal like none other. Over the years, God was not far off. In fact, He was there before either of us called.

Through the Word of God, He guided me. Through the spirit of discernment, He led me. Through faith, He ushered me into the presence of comfort, knowing He cares for and loves me like none other. Over the years, I felt through the Holy Spirit as though I was in a class of one—with the Lord as my greatest teacher.

To date, my personal heartache is teaching me and leading me into unknown territory. I must admit there is something exciting, intriguing yet scary about the journey that awaits me. But because I have a history with my Lord and Savior, the greater part of me trusts Him to guide and take me into my next chapter.

Stay tuned for updates.

Chapter Two

Rain, Rain Please Go Away

Henry Wadsworth Longfellow said, "Into each life some rain must fall." This quote has been spoken in many forums—some positive and some negative. In my humble opinion, truer words have never been spoken.

However, rain in and of itself can represent different concepts. Such as we need rain to grow, to stay fit, to nourish our bodies, to keep us healthy. When we open our thoughts to all the possibilities of how rain in general can benefit us, we can be reminded of the manifold blessings that come our way through our personal storms to make us stronger and our lives much richer.

When rain comes into our individual lives, we do not readily know what to expect from it. For some, it can seem more like a tropical storm, hurricane, tornado, or severe thunderstorm. What it means to you depends on your perspective.

Nevertheless, each individual must choose the particular route of his or her personal navigation. Some people view the aftermath of their storm as losing "everything" that mattered most to them, including their identities.

For others, it might mean the possibility of starting anew, because everything they once held dear no longer exists. Yet still, you will have those who are just lost in personal thoughts and are not sure about what to do in their new so-called normal. What is scary about this approach is that they sometimes unknowingly look in the wrong direction or to the wrong person for answers.

The world has a way of wanting you to rush into the new forum of lifestyle and new way of living without any downtime—never realizing your new world requires a process you never lived before. Before running full speed ahead into the unknown, there should always be clarity first.

Not only is this new way of living brand new, but it is also uncharted ground for anyone to explore. Everything has changed, and you may find yourself treading waters deeper than you can swim through. Therefore, you should tread lightly and intentionally.

To some degree, I try to consider unsolicited advice from professionals—or at least those who have some proof-positive, tested experience that rendered them successful. I avoid those whose advice has never been proven.

Often, when I am given random, spontaneous advice off the cuff, I quickly weed out the ill-willed advice from those who don't have a clue or experience about the suggested information they are providing.

Although no one can escape the rain that will come into all our lives, it is vital we make sure we are walking through our storms with our personal umbrellas—which is the Word of God for ourselves and not the opinion of others.

When walking through our personal storms and rains, this is not the time to look to ordinary people for guidance. It is not the time to draw our conclusions about the direction we think we should take for our lives, because every decision, right or wrong, has consequences.

Just like real life, if one is caught in a severe thunderstorm without the proper rain gear, it is quite possible for that unprepared individual to drown in the current. We are not talking about a few raindrops here and there. I am talking about flash flooding, when water can rise rapidly without a moment's notice, and it's too late to get out.

It is important to note that not all rainstorms are disastrous for your life. Sometimes, showers of rain are very necessary and useful.

There could be debris in our lives lying dormant in our hearts, minds, and thoughts that is of no intrinsic value to us. It merely clogs up space that could otherwise be useful.

We won't know it is there unless and until something dramatic or life-threatening happens to jolt us into real time. Then we notice and act on it, causing a change to emerge for our betterment.

Rain can also cause things to be rebuilt from a positive vantage point. It gives us an opportunity to explore things in our lives from a totally different angle than before.

Things could look bleak and obscured prior to the rain. Afterward, we can dance in the rain to different sounds and sights that caused us to grow and become alive because of the unique ways we grew from the rain.

While we are experiencing rain in our lives, we can use that opportunity to take personal inventory. What things are necessary to continue carrying? And what unnecessary things must we leave behind in our new journey?

I like to think of rain in my life as a refreshing concept. I find myself asking God to use the rain in my life as a refresher course and a time of renewal—whatever that might look like to Him for me.

I do not take that thought lightly. At first, the rain can be looked upon as sadness and heaviness. But I am learning that if I allow the rain to accomplish what it came into my life for, after a while, I know the sun will shine brightly again.

Rain can be utilized as a cleaning solution for all life's illnesses. After we have a good cry, our tears can act as a calming scent or solution that can affect our bodies and minds. They infuse in us a relaxing state to begin the process of thinking differently.

Our rainstorms can also relieve stressors from our lives if we allow them to. Sometimes even walking in the rain can be a beautiful distraction from anxiety that causes us to shift our focus. It often helps to make previous worries and cares feel less significant.

In my grieving process, several people simply hugged me and said, "Brenda, one of the most important things you can do for yourself now is to be kind to yourself and take all the time you need to grieve."

I found those words soothing and comforting to me—not that I needed anyone's permission. But I promised myself. During one of the most difficult and challenging rainstorms in my life thus far, I would not try to rush my pain. I would not force my emptiness to go away just so I could mark the dates off my calendar. I realized it would be necessary for me to embrace, cherish, and even appreciate each step for what it was worth to me.

I am even taking the time to pause during the rain to hold my head up and allow the raindrops to trickle down my head, face, and heart. To feel every emotion that comes with the pain and sorrow, because the life we shared together was authentic.

Audie was worth every drop.

Even while my heart is shattered into many tiny pieces as we speak, I understand God alone can put me back together in due time. The forward plans He has for my life are still in His divine motion.

During this process in my journey, His will for my life has become my will. I hope and trust that the personal plans He has for my life are those of prospering and being in good health. I continue striving to live for Him and reign with Him one day.

On June 3rd, 2024, at 5:00 a.m., I made up my mind that I was only going to believe God no matter what came. Even if the pain and sorrow I had to face knocked me to my knees, I knew it would be only Jesus that could take me through the process of being alone.

While the warm tears roll down my cheeks and my heart is broken, sometimes even now, I am unable to utter words loudly to pray.

I simply look up to Jesus and say in my mind, "Lord, only you know my pain level. Please take care of me through it all."

I have come to the conclusion that even after prayer, I have to choose to believe God and to take Him directly at His word. I do not have to beg Him, solicit His compassion, or try to move Him with my excellent speech. All that is necessary now in my life is to "only believe Him for the remainder of my days."

I am embracing the fact that, whether into my life comes rain, sleet, or shine, the Lord God Almighty is good at all times. It is His name alone that is worthy to be praised. I am assured He watches over His Word to perform it, and He does so with excellence.

It is God who has been and will continue to be my Strong Tower and my personal Prince of Peace. He has always been our Shelter and our Hiding Place. Since the transition of my beloved husband, I feel as though God is nearer to me now than ever before.

Even though I love the bright sunshine, strangely enough, the rain is slowly becoming my best friend. As I accept the rain into my life, I am pleasantly surprised just how much the rain washes away all the unnecessary cares and undue heartache I have endured for countless years.

Today, I was reminded of the scripture reference in 2 Corinthians 4:9-11 (KJV), "Persecuted, but not forsaken; cast down, but not destroyed; always bearing about in the body the dying of the Lord Jesus, that the life also of Jesus might be made manifest in our body. For we which live are always delivered unto death for Jesus' sake, that the life also of Jesus might be made manifest in our mortal flesh."

I am so very thankful to God for everything He has ever done for me and my family. For over sixteen-and-a-half years, He has delivered us. Watched over us. Shepherd us through every trial, testing, and hardship.

Every conceivable step of the way, God has been our Mountain Mover and our personal Deliverer. He has been our Stay and Healer. There is absolutely no one like Him. No one can ever compare to Him.

Another very important note about rain—if you have not started, please look at the rain in your life as a way and means of new beginnings. See it as a cleansing that refreshes, with the ability to wash away those things that no longer work for what is now necessary in your life.

Also, build for yourself a tribe or a village that will be there for you. One to pour into you and build a circle of hope and strength for you. Look for people who are positive and supportive of who you are and not just people who will say whatever they feel you want to hear. Trust me—you will need them to lean on when the rain comes.

From my personal experience, it is often too late to start building while you are in the rain. During the rainstorm, it can become quite difficult to know who's actually for you and who is simply nosy and curious about you.

You must also seek to have a very keen spirit of discernment to be aware of predators and scammers alike. Know that every potential smile can sometimes simply be a frown turned upside down, waiting for an opportunity to pounce and take advantage of your temporary heartache. My advice to anyone is not to make a move without involving God first.

Be determined, especially in your pain, to wait on God for concrete answers. My motto is, "If God is not speaking, I am not moving." And if the decisions I must make need an urgent "yes," then it is an automatic no. Do not be afraid to walk, if not run, away.

Look not unto the hills but unto Him from whom all your help comes. From the Lord who knows all there is to know about you, and allow only God to order your steps.

I realized if I am going to allow God to order my steps, I must be careful not to invite or include additional voices to plug in and have free rein over my decisions. God has great and specific plans for us that were orchestrated by Him alone.

We must trust the process of God even when the rain comes and stays for a while. Don't panic when the rain comes as a downpour, or if flooding ensues from the rain coming into our lives at the moment. When we learn to lean, trust, and rest in God, we can be assured we can still believe in the hand of God over our lives.

Even during the rain, we might sustain storm damage from debris. It is during those times when the rain brings harm to our physical property that we may also feel as though life isn't fair or that God

Himself doesn't care or see our suffering and our pain. But this is the time when we must learn how to press into what we know personally about God.

It is important to close the book on negativity and walk out by faith with what we believe about our relationship in Christ. We can stretch out in God and trust His promises that have been spoken over our lives—especially when we have seen Him deliver before.

Chapter Three

Self-Care is Vital

WHEN YOUR LIFE IS in crisis mode and you know for yourself, you cannot push further in your health, mental, spiritual, or financial state, this is the perfect time when you must stop, pull over, and get immediate help. Don't even think twice about it.

Self-care is bigger than a suggestion or a great idea! Self-care is urgent. Necessary. Vital. In fact, the very first thing one should do before trying to attend to others' wounds is to place yourself at the very top of your list of healing mechanisms.

Self-care is bigger than scheduling a spa day, getting a makeover, having a glass of wine with the girls, or even taking a day off from work here and there. Self-care is placing yourself first in your own life. Doing whatever it takes to make sure you are mentally, physically, emotionally, psychologically, spiritually, and financially whole from the inside out.

Remember—just because you are mobile does not mean you are mentally and emotionally ready or stable to be behind your natural or spiritual wheel to move full steam ahead.

In fact, I wholeheartedly believe when you are in a devastating or hurtful crisis mode, and your entire world has been rocked and turned upside down and shattered, the best thing you can do is stop and place everything around you on necessary pause. Turn all your attention to the matter at hand. You.

Don't think you need to explain why. Don't even look to anyone outside of yourself for answers. And please do not think others will understand. They may not listen to your pain—at least not for extended periods.

As people in general, we are not wired that way in and of ourselves. It seriously takes an act of God planting that seed of compassion, longsuffering, and genuine concern to place other's need before our own.

We are counters at heart, counting everything. We count how long we have been alive or the years since someone passed on. And we count how long we have been on the job, if we have a job. How long we have been married or divorced.

It's almost like an obsession, as if the pain and anguish we go through somehow lessens with age or time. I suppose it can, but I really believe the pain doesn't go away because of "time." Rather, it goes away because we accept that the change itself cannot be undone. We make the choice either to accept the new normal or remain stuck in the pain.

The change happens and we must accept that what has taken place is our new norm, which doesn't have to always mean the worst. It could possibly be for the good in the long run.

In the meantime, we have to trust God's process, which is not always easy to accept. Even when we have no clue how it may all turn out, we can reason that God's ways and thoughts are far greater than ours. Even when we are scared and doubtful, still we must cry out to him and ask him to take the wheel and guide us step-by-step along the way.

Self-care must be intentional and heartfelt. It must be one of the most selfless things you can do for yourself. As life happens, it is important not to live in denial or in a make-believe state of mind, as if you can handle everything by yourself.

For me, God has become a priority. First place. Primary. The total source of reliance. He has become my Rock. My Stabilizer and my Anchor whom I can totally depend upon. I am lost without him.

The self-care I need is not merely busying myself with various things that simply occupy my time or fill in a vacant space. Self-care is about personally checking in with yourself and making sure you provide yourself with the tools and resources you need to remain whole both inside and outside.

It is about doing only those things that fulfill you and make you relevant in the moment. No, this is not being selfish. This is being aware and observant of what you need and being confident about how to make sure you lay hold of it.

Self-care is about self-discovery of your purpose and where those roads lead in your personal walk. It is about getting to know your strength and weaknesses and embracing them both. Not trying to make them equal, because that is not necessary. Rather finding the correct balance when one or the other shows up and stays longer than intended.

Self-care is not being afraid to admit or to acknowledge you are scared, nervous, confused, lost, fallen off the grid, disappointed, hurt, angry, or even sad, because all of these emotions are a part of our makeup.

They don't make us weak; they make us real and relevant. They make us human and show that all these attributes should lead us back to our Maker. He can order our steps to make sure we arrive to our next level in one piece.

It is perfectly okay to stop, sit quietly, and take deep breaths before making another move. Never push yourself or allow others to rush you into making knee-jerk decisions or sudden moves—especially those you are unsure of.

While it is vital to get the necessary help or self-care you need, it is equally important that you seek God. At least seek godly counseling about getting the correct and beneficial sources that bring about the appropriate healing necessary for you, so you heal properly and in a timely and safe manner.

Often when life has thrown you into a traumatic crisis, people outside the scope of your pain will try their best to care for you, help you, pray for you, and assist in your healing process. That's a wonderful thing. Still, trust in the Lord and lean not unto your own understanding.

However, this is the precise time you need to remain true to who you know you are. As difficult and challenging as this time will be, you can do it. But you must stop and try to put everything into its proper perspective.

You do not have to make rash or irrational decisions about anything. These are dark times, hurtful, and possibly grieving emotional times. Only you have to accept and take personal ownership of each day and decision.

In that moment, you don't have to strain to make sense out of what quite frankly doesn't make sense. It is important to remember your life as you once knew it has just shifted and changed drastically forever.

No matter what, it has changed in ways and manners that will never be the same. No matter how much you love, miss, or cherish that person, thing, or relationship, it has now changed. There is no going back.

It is important to accept that you do not have to rush forward. Stay in the moment and allow it to minister to you. You may feel as though you are going to break, or not make it through, but in time, you will.

Another very important factor to accept is that during the next season or chapter of your life, from time-to-time, depending upon what state of crisis mode you are in, fear, doubt, or second-guessing yourself can become your greatest enemy.

If you do not recognize where the doubt is coming from, you may easily fall prey to the pressure of it all and fall into its trappings that whisper, "You are not going to make it!"

Take your time to rest in God. Allow His full presence to hover over your every move. Talk to Him about everything you are feeling, experiencing, and thinking. Your conversation with Him will remain safe, sound, and therapeutic.

I personally found in my days of challenges, God is there for me during every step of the way. He promised never to leave us or forsake us. Knowing that in my heart was, and still is, priceless for me today.

Trust Him in that promise. Don't rush through the heartache. In fact, take your much needed time and take ownership of those moments. Allow those emotions and sometime emptiness to provide for your total healing and necessary breakthroughs you need to forge ahead.

There is no limit on how often you can cry out to God. Please cry out to Him with your whole heart and tell Him all about it. Of course, He already knows, but this is your time to be forthright with Him and vulnerable.

Don't be overly concerned with whether your conversation with him is in proper form. He knows how to unscramble the eggs to what you are trying to say.

Be patient with yourself in crisis mode. Oftentimes, there are decisions that need to be made and paperwork that needs to be signed. You may not feel comfortable dealing with those decisions at the moment. Allow the Holy Spirit to lead and guide you through the entire process. I can promise you, He will.

Be very prayerful, alert, and deliberate when moving forward with the decisions you make. Please seek wise counsel from someone you know and respect that you know loves God. Choose one who respects and has genuine concern for you that will walk with you through the things that matter.

Ask God to help you be clear, concise, extremely sober-minded, and fully aware of what is taking place at any given moment. But especially when making those decisions that can alter the rest of your life.

Be careful to stay in touch with your emotions. Should you feel any type of pressure to commit to something you are unsure about, don't. Walk away if you must, but do not allow yourself to feel as though you need to make a decision at that moment.

Don't fall for the pressured sales call or the must do it right now scheme. Pray for the spirit of discernment and refuse to move if you do not have the peace of God to do so. Remember that the wrong choices we make can have irrevocable cost afterward. You are the one left holding the negative consequences of it all.

Absolutely pray about everything and be confident in God's response about what you have been praying. God will get in the midst of the situations you are facing and cradle you while you are journeying through it. No matter how long the journey may take, go willingly with God who has all the answers you could possibly need.

If for some reason you decide to seek out help on your own, with the leadership of God, please ask Him to order your steps. Then be in tune with His guidance from the beginning until the end.

My advice is when you go to speak with this individual, do not be afraid to take someone else that you are close to with you.

Don't do all the talking and please do not share too much information about your personal journey too soon. Let them earn your trust and respect. Please understand that everyone you may be talking with does not have your best interest at heart.

Always take precautions by being extra cautious no matter what is going on. Never second guess yourself. If you do not have a positive gut feeling, please do not feel the need to ignore it and move full speed ahead in the process.

Even when you feel comfortable talking with someone you may have been recommended to, never move forward until God has provided you the peace to go ahead.

Do not just seek help. It must be the right type of help that will prove itself beneficial in the end. Caring and compassionate help. This type of help and recovery can only come from the Lord. He alone is the only true Helper.

When your mind, body, and soul is in a true crisis mode, nothing else matters in that moment. You do not have the physical strength to put one foot forward. You may be able to hear conversations, but you are unable to differentiate the content being said to you. Those critical moments may break your decision-making choices.

When you are under great pressure, this is not the time to push yourself beyond your human strength. You do not have anything to prove to anyone. Therefore, it is okay to put the brakes on and stop until you can operate clearly.

During stressful moments and events in our life, we are more than likely pulled into several directions without any idea of where we are headed. One minute we appear to be in control, while the next we are discombobulated and turned around in need of guidance.

Stressors in our lives can bring about all sorts of other medical issues we didn't see coming. We don't see the unhealthy weight loss or the loss of hair due to constant worry. We don't recognized the inability to get a good night's sleep, because we are too busy stressing over what might happen.

Sometimes it is possible to look in the mirror and not recognize ourselves. We may wonder what the old self looked like, because it has been so long since we last checked.

You may ask yourself if you are pleased with the person staring back at you in the mirror. Would both of you agree with the findings that you see?

So often as women, we are wonderful at allowing ourselves to believe whatever we are comfortable with, admitting anything as factual information in the moment.

We are not always good about admitting our weaknesses out loud. Sometimes, to admit our flaws, whether done privately or with a close friend, can be too much to bear or say. We do not want to run the risk of being judged.

We have difficulty saying no, and we take on way too much in the first place. We stretch ourselves entirely too thin to our detriment. Often, we allow ourselves to take on others' burdens without being totally informed about the totality or the scope of it all.

We busy ourselves with a motherlode of work, chores, errands, projects, and weekend events. The workload never stops, and we struggle beneath the unnecessary load of things we were never supposed to carry.

We forget that the Bible tells us our bodies are the temple of the Lord. We should take care in how we steward it. The only time we stop and take notice is usually when our bodies shut down in the midst of it all, and we cannot move any further.

As a woman, I have been found guilty of taking on more than my share of one project too many. Not knowing when to say no, I cannot handle another thing on my plate for the fear of letting someone down.

In other instances, I allowed others to guilt me into saying yes when everything within me screamed don't do it. Even still, somehow we have been given a guilt trip early on to believe we must become all things to every person. We subliminally think that somehow we are supposed to do it all at all times. No downtime or rest for the weary, we become a one-stop shop no matter what.

It makes us feel weak or not confident enough to make good decisions about our lives. Therefore, we speak positively on the outside, but inside we negatively lie to ourselves about what or who we think we really are.

One of the most important and necessary takeaways I have found is the method to living our best lives. Take full ownership of our authentic selves. The only way to do that is by spending quality, real time with ourselves.

Take the opportunity, believe it or not, to spend time alone and meditate upon the goodness of God in your life. Don't be in a hurry to get through the moment. In fact, take in every waking moment as though it is a precious gift. Because—actually, it is.

Learn how to be kind, compassionate, and loving with lessons life teach you. Embrace the hurts, disappointments, let downs, failures, and flaws. For they each came to impart into us the next vital piece of the puzzle for our life's mission.

Self-care has more to do with self-awareness and self-evolvement. When we learn to embrace our so-called failures like we hold dear our upswings as though they were trophies we have won, then and only then do we really began to grow and get to know ourselves inside and out.

Fear can also be our greatest cheerleader—especially when faced with the largest obstacles in our journey. Fear can teach us many valuable and crucial lessons about who we were created to be in the wake of triumph.

Nothing ventured and I can guarantee you there will be nothing gained. You must learn how to embrace failure wholeheartedly if you ever stand a chance of being successful.

If you want to know how good success will look on you, try looking into the mirror or your past. It will provide you with a resounding response to how well you handled your failures, because the outcome will mimic the same results until you have learned how to hold both with dignity and grace.

Self-care does not indicate that we travel our personal journeys alone. It simply means we are not too prideful to ask for and receive help from others who care enough to help us carry the load.

Self-care recognizes that God never intended for us to ignore Him in our weariness and our moments of frailty. What is very important to remember is that God desires to help us at every interval.

God is not just a random helper or someone willing to participate in the help. He alone is the Present Help that sticks closer than a brother. God is the real deal. More than able. More than capable. God is the Constant, the Forever answer to all our problems if we would just surrender our will to Him.

In the world today, most people take issue with surrendering their wills to anyone for fear of losing control over their lives. But God isn't just any old person. He is the only way, the truth, and the life. Without Him, we cannot do anything. Nothing. Not a chance.

For me, the word surrender does not indicate losing control but rather placing my trust, faith, confidence, and belief in the hands of someone that doesn't just have a good idea for my life. But the One with the plan that would cause me to live my best life.

Self-care is about making good choices that will assure you of living intentional. A life well lived and thought out. A life that involves prayer, purpose, and reasoning.

Please understand that self-care will not happen by merely wishing and hoping. Quite the contrary. It can only happen when we make healthy choices that cause us to live in real time and with conscious efforts. So our intent matches up with our will to see our drive, desire, and commitment make it come to fruition.

To begin the process of self-care, we must take a long hard look at what dynamics look like and be willing to take full ownership of our role or part in the healing process. We can ask God what He wants us to do to allow our healing to come forth.

Chapter Four

Considerate of Others' Pain

OFTEN, WHEN HEARTACHE HAPPENS to someone due to the devastating loss of a loved one or the loss of a job or something important to them, it leaves a gaping hole in his or her heart that could take weeks, months, or perhaps years before it is mended.

During those most challenging times it can be unbearable if not devastating to the person in the midst of personal grief. Especially if that person doesn't understand those who surround you must have a stake in your wellbeing—not just for the moment, but for the future as well.

In your time of grief, countless pieces of advice come at you from all directions. And because you are not in the head space or fully mindful of it all, you may be unsure of what is really best for you.

Every grieving person has the right to grieve according to individual pain. Pain is so very personal and intimate. It is not a time to be ignored or taken for granted. We should not be afraid to pay close attention to what those emotions bring to us and the vital lessons to learn through it all.

In fact, this is not the time to compare your grief with that of others. This is not a comparison moment to question, challenge, or stand in judgment. It is important to remember that everyone's grief is personal, intimate, and different. It deserves respect from others who look on.

No one should try to gauge or set a timer on another's grief, because it can only add insult and salt to an already fresh wound in the early stages of human survival. And the last thing an individual in pain needs is an untrained and uncertified counselor to provide them with unwarranted and sometimes unwanted ill advice.

What is necessary and always appreciated is prayers and compassion for those individuals who struggle just to wrap their minds and thoughts around what is now their new norm.

Another important and vital piece of advice I would offer is not to expect too much, too soon from those who are grieving. It is impossible for them to return every phone call, to respond to every text, or to remember who brought what or came by to see them.

Please understand they do care. They are appreciative of your genuine love and support, but in the moment, they are in a zone that is uncharted and fresh for them. They are fortunate if they can remember their name and telephone number. Please remember that they need appropriate time to heal and begin the process of a whole new world. They need time to become acclimated to their brand-new journey. Trust me, it is a lot to undertake.

While it is difficult for others to find the right words to say to those who are hurting, please know we appreciate the thought of your genuine prayers and kindness. Some people are left speechless and have difficulty coming to grips with the pain or loss they personally feel.

For the minutes, hours, and days after the loss, those individuals are often left with only the memories, heartaches, and unbearable pain that fills their loneliness. They have a dire need to fill the hole left in their hearts. As they scramble to make sense of what has no logic in the days ahead, they can be left with their thoughts, sense of uncertainty, and the struggle to remain focused.

For the individual experiencing the loss, it is important for others around them to understand that they do not have all or any answers. They are doing enough just to remain sane themselves.

Remember, they are not only dealing with a tremendous loss but also the sharp new reality that they will never ever see their loved one on this earth again. Their pain is fresh, their wound is open, and they are really going through a harsh time.

They are so appreciative and thankful for the family and friends who are there for them in any way possible. Moreso for those who stay close long after the funeral services are over.

For the individual experiencing personal loss, this is totally new territory for them to explore one day at a time. They have no earthly idea of just how that territory will be navigated. So, much prayer and patience is valued during that time.

Loss of any type can be beyond overwhelming to say the least. It takes time and a whole lot of prayer just to place one foot before the other. Please remember that to the hurting, unnecessary and unfair judgment is the last thing anyone needs.

They struggle to find the proper footing they were once accustomed to. They search for answers but find only additional questions left unresolved. They hope with all their heart they will wake up and find out it was only a dream. Even still, we must all strive to use restraint and think about our comments and actions before we respond or blurt out questions or responses. Put ourselves in the shoes of the distraught or hurting person in need of comfort and support.

I would like to think most people are sincere when they provide words of encouragement after a loved one dies, or an accident happens. However, others need to give much thought to, and perhaps pray first, before uttering a word or making suggestions or insinuations of any kind. If your words are not going to provide encouragement, comfort, peace, or support in the long run, please consider whether it should be said at all. If possible, try to treat others as you would want someone to treat you when your time of pain comes.

It is not difficult to understand when you stop and think about it. In that moment, the hurting person is often distraught, overwhelmed, and living in survivor mode. The very last thing a hurting person needs are inquisitive spectators standing by to inflict additional heartache.

Much consideration should be given to the person grieving. Most of the time, when bad news is given to the families about a loved one, the thought they will not see that individual again is so traumatizing they may become unable to move forward for years afterward.

During someone else's loss, this is not the time to start sharing all the personal and private things currently happening in your life. If possible, try to remain in the moment and assist the grieving family to cope with love and genuine tenderness. Not only should compassion and empathy be demonstrated at times like these, but sincere care and sincerity should be as well. Refrain from asking the grieving family things like, "How did they die? or How old were they?" As if the age lessens that individual's pain.

It is always encouraging to put the grieving family's comfort first rather than making them feel worst with comments that are unnecessary, unwarranted, and quite frankly, ungodly.

Another good point of reference is to follow the grieving family cues. If it becomes evident they would like to talk about the details, and the family chooses to share more details into what, why, and when, then follow their lead.

One of the reasons why precaution should be taken into consideration before, during, and after a funeral is that long after the service has been completed, personal grief is just getting started. Planning a funeral is all that individual can do to maintain their sanity and simply get through it. During this very sensitive time in their lives, they need prayers, comforting words, and the sincerity of all who love them to assist in processing it all.

It is so sad when others use their energy to judge those hurting or grieving. When every little thing they are going through is being reviewed under the microscope, some stand on the sideline and put their mouths of personal opinions on the grieving family. They judge everything from how long the funeral was to what the grieving widow wore.

Even more sad, when they see the grieving family member later, one of the first things they say is, "Oh, I have been praying for you and your family."

There is nothing wrong with showing others, especially those who are grieving, grace and mercy. Be big enough to think positively about them rather than judge them on every oversight they may be going through.

As the old saying goes, when oversights are made by that family, be quick to charge mistakes to their head and not to their heart. Don't become offended as if they overlooked you intentionally.

It is important to know and try to understand that grief is real—especially to those individuals in pain and sometimes disbelief. When a loved one passes away, many necessary and difficult decisions must be made at a moment's notice. They do not have the capacity to remember every tiny thing.

Sometimes during heartache, it may be one or two individuals within that family planning the entire funeral without any help or assistance. This person can experience stress beyond measure and often looks at some of the most pertinent details until everything is over.

No one should be offended or angry because the funeral details or notifications to them were overlooked. They may not have been made aware of the death of that loved one. Please do not take it personally or be offended that you weren't personally reached out to. Mistakes and oversight can happen during these sensitive times.

In other case scenarios, some individuals cannot help themselves from providing specific timeframes for how long an individual should grieve. Just refrain. Not only insensitive, this is often unsolicited advice. There is never an appropriate time to provide others with a timeframe for personal grief. It will take as long as it takes for them to grieve.

Therefore, do not judge. Rather, offer truthful and helpful support if needed. Be open to the fact that every death is different. Every pain is different, and no one should be giving specific instructions on just how long another person's pain may take before they remotely walk in their healing. Only God can prescribe that kind of medicine.

The world is full of angry, disgruntle people who want to see others in disparity and bitterness, hopelessness and a pitiful state of mind. After all, misery loves company. The grieving individual must find strength in God to push through and keep their head up, looking unto Jesus—the true Author and Finisher of our soul.

Jesus is the only true way maker and the authentic author of our everlasting hope. He is the only One we should be looking to in times of trouble and loss. In fact, the best time to seek Him is in the good times of our lives. So when the dark days and nights come, we can trust in His track record and be fully persuaded He will keep us in His perfect peace.

As a people of God, when we truly honor the Word of God in our individual lives, it will be reflected in how we love and serve others. Especially when we see our brothers and sisters suffering or dealing with insurmountable pain and heartache.

Love in and of itself is the most powerful and beautiful reflection of God. Most importantly, we walk it out before men. Not so people will glorify us, but rather so Christ's name will be seen and given its proper place in the earth and in the lives of those who may not know Christ exists.

Having gone through personal years with my spouse as his caregiver, I have come to see and experience firsthand how patient true love can be. I thank God He allowed me to explore the many depths and variances of what it means to linger and wait with gladness.

I am by no means suggesting that being a caregiver is not challenging on both the patient and the caregiver. Believe you me, one has to truly be made to carry out both assignments. But at the end of the day, they are both possible through Christ.

To the people who are merely peeking through the windows of others without understanding or having compassion, they are clueless about what I am speaking. Without genuine love for Christ, no one can truly serve in any capacity as it relates to Kingdom building.

Chapter Five

Take Your Time

WHEN YOU ARE EXPERIENCING serious heartache, the very last thing you want is to take things slow. If anything, you want to hit the gas and accelerate out of that camp as quickly as you can.

As a matter of fact, not only do you want the pain and sorrow out of your life as quickly as possible, you never want any remnants of the pain to settle in, let alone linger. Inwardly you may feel like, "Pain, please go somewhere else. Anywhere else besides here in my life. I've already been through enough."

Personally, I want to learn from my pain. I can honestly say that throughout my lifetime, I actually have. In fact, if I were totally transparent, I would have to say pain has caused a lot of my maturity and spiritual growth.

In time, I have learned the art of waiting and lingering—not stewing in my pain or allowing it to overtake me. Seeking the unadulterated truth from God in those bleak and uncharted waters in my life led me to His truth. It provided not just relief for me, but breakthroughs from those old hurts and shackles that kept me boggled down.

I have heard the adage that time can heal all wounds. I am not absolutely sure about that part. Unless you are willing to do the work to release the old hurts and wounds and allow the willingness of forgiveness and regret to move you forward, the only thing time will do is cause you to become incubated. There, you are stuck in the hurt for longer periods while feeling miserable.

In life, time can be a formidable benefactor for us against our arch enemy. Using time as a positive force can serve as a guidepost by which we can allow ourselves to seek the necessary help we need to move forward. Time can lead us to a more productive life and lifestyle, or to prolong true joy and happiness. Because we are afraid to deal with the trauma, we remain stuck in it for a while.

The negative side is what I call wasted time. In other words, time spent trying my best to figure out the what, when, and why of how I arrived at the place of pain I am in. Focusing on the agony or the result of why something didn't work out as I planned only wastes time better spent healing.

Taking a good long stare at our world today, everywhere you look is speed and the need for more haste. Everywhere you turn, the majority of drivers on the road appear in a hurry to get to their "next" wherever that road may lead. As long as they arrive at their destination safely, or not, they exude, "get out of my way."

One of the main problems about that mindset is that the world isn't just about one person or one particular thing. It includes others, and all people matter.

It is so important to slow down and take your time in general. It is necessary to think for yourself about decisions you make and the consequences following those decisions. Determine the reasoning or validation for those decisions and the possible outcomes. No decision should ever be taken lightly or without prayer and much thought. While it may be considerate to ask others for their advice, never allow their final word to be the catchall over your life. That gives away your power to think for yourself and make sure the outcome is the absolute best for your life overall.

Taking your time does not include a rush job to get past or over the subliminal hurdle you may feel you need to jump over right now. Taking your time is giving yourself permission to stop. Think. Pray. Wait and then move forward cautiously with wisdom.

Taking your time means you have put in the necessary work, resources, effort, and thought it takes to get out of the pain. But it also means achieving the intended outcome you personally want to see and live with.

Never allow an uninformed party to navigate the direction of your life. Always pray and seek the counsel of someone who has demonstrated Christ in their life to talk and share your heart with. In other words, you haven't just heard them talk the talk, but you have witnessed them walking the walk and delivering a wholesome outcome.

Time for some people makes them extremely nervous and less confident—especially in their decision making. They may feel if they are unable to move quickly without too much thought that they are on top of the matter rather than dragging their feet.

It appears the entire universe is in a rush to go, go, go. Only to end up most often at a dead uninformed end that leads to nowhere. Patience is no longer a virtue, and politeness is almost a thing of the past. Tension is at an all-time high, and courtesy is almost nonexistence.

Even though it can be challenging to wait and trust the process, at the end of the day, the conclusion is going to be a result of the choices we set into motion. The outcome of it all will either be one of two things: life or death. Therefore, it is imperative I take my time and choose to select wisely.

I don't know about anyone else, but it seems to me just about everything around me is changing. And not all of it is for the betterment. From time-to-time, after the death of my beloved spouse, my path has crossed with individuals who knew both of us.

They'll ask, "Hey, Brenda, how's it going?"

To which my response nine times out of ten will be, "All is well."

This response is usually followed up with, "But how are you really doing?"

I know most of the time, if not all, the follow-up response is met with, "Are you sure?"

Are they fishing for more specific details, because the latter cannot be true? But the truth of the matter, at least for me, all is indeed well.

Now, I am by no means saying I do not miss the love of my life in every instance. But I am allowing the love of God to teach me how to rest in Him while living with loneliness and separation.

Time is a wise teacher, and it will absolutely teach us if we are willing to learn and trust God's process for our lives. Pain ordered by God is never allowed into our lives to destroy us or cripple us. Instead, time serves as a gentle reminder that life is very precious and should never be wasted or taken for granted.

Most people become nervous, antsy, and fidgety, especially when we are hurdling into the unknown. Daily, I witness conversations between people trying to convince others to hurry up and make a decision about this or that, or to live their lives in a manner that only makes sense to them. The rush to live in the fast lane is clearly on. I have a problem with this type of thinking. There never appears to be an opportunity to consider the decisions without thoughts of the aftermath or consequences that always follow. I mean, after all, what's the real rush?

The average person is forever chasing after the next big thing or the next discovery, never allowing much time for their lives or tender moments that are special and dear to them. Life is meant to be lived to the fullest. I believe life is such a precious and incredible gift God gives to each of us, because he so desires for us not to simply exist, but to actually live out who he created us to be. Our lives are meant to max out **our godly design and** to live the best version of ourselves.

While it is understandable that no one wants to linger or prolong their pain, they do not get the connection of why they have to endure it, either. As human beings, we often look at our lives through our thinking and imagination. We forget God's thoughts are so, so, so far above ours. His ways are undeniably above anything we can remotely think or imagine. If we would only relinquish our will and powerless strength and lean on God for our total understanding, we would be more able to stand against the wiles and evilness of this world. When we take our time and don't get in a hurry to know everything, we would learn how to trust in the One who knows everything, planned everything and spoke everything into existence. We would be so much better.

The enemy of this world wants nothing more than for us to rush through life making irrational, knee-jerk decisions based upon half-truths and minimal direction. He does not want you and me to seek wise, godly counsel—to sleep on the idea before we make a move.

Because he already knows if we choose to wait and pray about it, more likely than not, the outcome of our decision will be turned for betterment, and our results will be healthier and beneficial.

Chapter Six

Everything Matters

As my life continues to mature in my daily walk with Jesus, I am finding out that absolutely everything matters in one way or the other. It is almost like putting together a pattern of sorts.

I imagine a seamstress preparing to make a dress or skirt from scratch without a pattern before them. All they have to rely on is their imagination. Everything concerning the outcome of their finished product depends upon how well they can visualize what they want the finished work to look like.

For this to happen, the seamstress must concentrate on what they are doing, remain focused on every aspect of the garment, and make sure every detail of their vision is followed precisely. Not one part of the overall outcome must be overlooked or abandoned if they expect to get the results they are hoping for.

In my personal life, I see it the same way. If I want to move forward out of the dark, dismal, hurtful, frustrating days of my life, I must first envision greater days ahead for me. I must believe my better days are really before me and that I can actually lay hold to those days and times within my grasp.

I must believe that if I set my mind upon things that are good, that are pure, that are honest and right, with the help of my faith and my belief in God, I can tunnel through and get to the other side in "due time" and on schedule. I'm able to do so with the understanding that the most important component in this goal is a real and intentional process. Not just to arrive at the appointed time, but also to enjoy the journey of getting there.

Most of us become frustrated, irritated, and agitated to the point that we quit too soon. The journey upheavals in our lives don't make sense, or it doesn't feel comfortable along the way—especially when we cannot figure things out on our own.

If the journey to us isn't obvious and in a hurry, we are over it already. We move on without understanding the very thing that could have been designed to grow us in areas beneficial to us. But they could also establish our lives in greater measure.

Believe it or not, it matters how I think, what I am thinking about, what I allow to enter my ear gate, and what thoughts live rent free in my head and heart. It matters what I believe and what or who I am putting my hope and trust in. It matters what lies I allow to guide and mentor me.

The words I speak out of my mouth matter. The lies I listen to as well as the lies I tell myself matter. How I respond to negative information matters. The company I keep matters. The friends I share my time with matter.

The dreams and hopes I have for my life matter. Whether I follow them or abandon them in mid stride matters at the end of the day. They all matter. If I care too much about who likes me, loves me, hates me, or merely tolerates me and doesn't celebrate me—all of that matters.

Why? Because it will have an influence upon the outcome of how I live and if I make the right or wrong choices that could prove costly for me in the end. Coming to the conclusion that everything matters helps avoid the unnecessary pitfalls and regretful moments that could plague me for the rest of my life.

When I look back over some of the younger years of my life, I realize I lived it with a totally different mindset. For the most part, I did not often take into considerations how my choices were affecting me. Perhaps I only focused on the decision before me I thought I needed to make. I didn't wait and pray about it. I didn't always give it extra thought. I didn't ask the necessary questions I should have. I simply relied on the salesperson's interpretation of why I should consider their opinion or knowledge. About why I needed what they were selling in my life at the time.

Looking over some of the decisions, I realized I gave too much strength and power to others who I thought really cared or knew what was best for me. I cared, at times, too much about making sure everyone was happy or comfortable around me before my own needs or happiness were considered. I tried to show them I loved them—perhaps more than they accepted true happiness for themselves. After many years of this behavior, I had to accept that it cost me dearly mentally, physically, and definitely financially.

It took a toll on my mental ability over the years to let go of the hurts and allow the healing balm of the Lord to heal me from the open wounds and the scarring left in the aftermath. Caused by those individuals who said often that they loved me and wanted the very best for me, but they really didn't in the long run.

Looking back, I see it more clearly now. Their "love" usually came with a potential price tag or with the connotation that, "If you really love me, then you will have no problem doing this or that for me without any questions whatsoever."

Even though most of the time, I was not in a financial position to assist with the needs or demands of others who promised to pay me back, I surrendered my will to theirs. I hoped against hope this favor or meeting their need would prove how much I loved them and cared about meeting their needs. I hoped they would see that I was trying to express my genuine love to them, hoping they would one day return the same sentiments of kindness to me. Unfortunately, for some of them, that day still has not come.

As you could probably guess, the outcome yielded the polar opposite. You see, over time I came to realize most empty pitchers can never be filled when there is a hole in the bottom. It is up to the owner to recognize the defect and stop using the pitcher, hoping against hope this defective product would yield better or different results.

It is inevitable that hurt people hurt others. I suppose that sometimes the hurt is not always intentional, but it can be deliberate. There is a difference between the two.

Being spiritually intentional involves being consciously and thoughtfully aware of directing our actions and our words to encourage others. It means being mindful of our attitudes and our priorities rather than coasting through life passively—as if we do not have to give an account for our thoughts, actions, or deeds.

When something is done intentionally, most often it refers to making choices and plans aligned with godly principles and values. These will not only bring about a specific outcome for ourselves but for others involved. When our intentions are done through the positive lens of following Christ, then and only then is our spiritual work or intention used to set goals for healing, change, or manifestation for the betterment of all involved.

To be intentional in our spiritual growth, there must be a sincere desire for true change and better outcomes for personal overall health and wealth. When we are deliberate, we are being thoughtful in our actions, making choices that align with God's will, and cultivating a cautious mindset that can assist us in experiencing a life of purpose and fulfillment.

Another important factor I would like to mention relates to understanding that everything matters. And how we look at time, especially the time given us to live on the earth, should always be at the top of our human radar.

Some individuals may look at time as being all theirs, and they can use it however they want. They believe everything is about them. Everything revolves around them, and sadly, they may even believe no one can possibly live without them.

What a very sad and tragic devastating lie to believe. Not only does everything matter, but everyone matters. E-v-e-r-y o-n-e matters. People are not an afterthought. People are not just extra body parts. They are entire human beings—living, breathing, thriving, and fully operational all by the sheer grace and mercy of God. We are imperative to the body of Christ and vital to the Kingdom's work here on earth. And we are necessary to each other.

Time is one of the most gracious commodities we have ever received in our entire lifetime. It is precious and priceless. We should treat it as an extravagant, beautiful jewel we could not afford to purchase with all the money in the world.

God is specific, and He created us with a unique identity that will never be duplicated. It cannot be exchanged for better or greater, because what He created us to be is matchless. No mere man can improve on it.

When we treasure what gifts or gifting have been placed in our care and responsibility, our hands, our knowledge, and our purpose, we will look at time differently. We will become more grateful and appreciative of exactly who we are and how we measure and mete out our time. Not by comparing ourselves to others, but to God's design for our individual lives.

It is so important never to compare ourselves to another human being that exemplifies the same flaws, bad habits, mistakes, emotions, downfalls, and errors we are subject to make on any given day. We are to take our cues from God and Him alone. At times, we care entirely too much about how others see us, if they see us, if they accept us, and if they deem us worthy of their time.

If this is your personal stance, I challenge you today—stop right now. Quit casting your important pearls to the uncaring swine who cannot stop you from being the very best version of yourself.

Chapter Seven

New Boundaries for the Journey Ahead

IN TODAY'S SOCIETY, IT can be quite a challenge to know when applying boundaries vs. barriers come into play. On the one hand, we don't want to offend anyone, but at the same time, we don't like being taken total advantage of either.

Unfortunately for some of us, we don't necessarily know exactly where to draw the line at what is considered okay and what is borderline intrusive or oversharing. One of the last things we need is to share too much of ourselves or things that matter to us, only to have it come back later and be thrown in our faces.

Sometimes, when we are sharing information in the moment, we may feel a twinge of uneasiness. Maybe everything within us is screaming, "Stop! That's enough." There are moments when we take it too far and regret it soon thereafter.

If we just pay attention to the person we are sharing with, we can often tell whether they are for us or merely snooping for more information to judge us by. The bottom line is when our personal space is invaded and not respected the first time, those signs should not be overlooked or ignored.

When you feel disrespected and judged by the way you choose to live, it should not become the decision making of someone outside the scope of who you are. Someone else's opinion of you should never become the conclusion over your life one way or the other.

Those nuances should be addressed in a way that establishes a clear-cut path to personal expectations in your life of what a "true friend" or acquaintance should be without a detailed reason. Your boundaries are absolutely yours to hold dear without anyone else's validation or approval. Simply allowing other's strong will and opinionated thoughts of you to finagle, twist, and cause you to change your mind and go in a different direction is all up to you.

Boundaries are not going to come easily. They have to be understood by the individual first. They must be attainable and realistic. They must be meted or measured in such a way you can be committed yet adjustable when life happens. And it will.

Just in case you may or may not have noticed, all around us in the world today, all sorts of things wait to detour the plans God has for us. All night and all day, there are thousands upon thousands of dollars spent on advertisements to persuade us not to follow God's intended plan.

For instance, there used to be a time you had to physically go to a car dealership to purchase a car. You had to talk with a salesman, test drive the car, and sit there for hours, nervous, sweating, wringing your hands, knees knocking from fear, fingers crossed, praying God would grant our wish to walk out of that dealership with our wish of 'a new ride.'

But marketing departments figured out a way to invade us through the mere world of persuasion. We do not need to leave home, because it's an inconvenience. They will bring the car to our doorstep. We just sit at home at the dining room table or in our recliner. With the push of a few buttons, the car could potentially be delivered to our front door within hours.

Through their research, they discovered consumers are more likely to purchase more or quickly if we are distracted or caught up in the moment by the ease of it all. We don't have to think long or be hounded by pushy salesmen. We can simply make these decisions all by our lonesome. By doing this on our own, the vendor or the owner is hoping while we are "in charge," we may not notice hidden costs in the agreement. They show us only our final cost.

So, they distract us with many bells and whistles under the false pretense of our convenience, and we fall for the trick every time—sometimes with an over-exaggerated APR we cannot afford to pay. But we cannot take it back, because we have already signed on the dotted line.

Boundaries are not a negative thing in and of themselves. In fact, they are more important than we think. Setting the appropriate boundaries can shield us from undue heartache and countless years of unnecessary pain and degradation. It can spare us disappointments, discontentment, and a host of unnecessary mistakes that can haunt us later in life—especially when we are unable to see what's ahead or just around the proverbial corner.

When we refuse to invest in boundaries for our lives, we don't realize it. But we are potentially setting ourself up for hurtful rejections, lies, jealousy, misunderstandings, and quite possibly going in the wrong direction for our lives.

Take, for instance, when we refuse to set appropriate boundaries, that gives others the impression nothing is off limits. No matter the subject, no matter how supposedly private a situation is, others may feel as though they should be privy to the ends and outs of what's happening in our lives without question. And when you no longer want to share, they may feel betrayed or think they are being rejected for no reason. Even though they have "always" been there for you they may claim now you are leaving them out.

They are hurt, confused, angry, and in disbelief. All of a sudden, it may seem as though "you have suddenly changed," and their friendship is no longer warranted, valued, or appreciated.

Remember—setting boundaries does not require permission to do so. However, it does require a made-up mind about how much permission you give yourself to grow and live your best life without other's input or unsolicited advice.

When setting boundaries of any kind, they should never be entered into haphazardly. They should be very carefully considered and even prayed over. The decisions you make can and will affect others around you. In that regard, it is necessary to give lots of thought, clarity, and great discernment to why the boundaries you may or may not set in place are the best ones for you and for those they will affect.

Before deliberately shutting others out of your life, please make sure you have done your homework and due diligence. Make sure this is the right move in your life for right now and for the right reasons.

As I have mentioned, no matter what final decision you make related to setting boundaries, always allow God to be a part of the equation from start to finish. He can and will make all the difference in the outcome of it all.

When we are willing to set spiritual boundaries, we are not just crossing our fingers and hoping it will work out. We can seek the help and guidance of someone who knows us intimately inside and out. Someone who cares for us deeply and wants us to live our best lives in full throttle will respect those boundaries without question. In fact, when we have boundaries, there will still be obstacles and incidents we will have to contend with. However, with God's guidance, we can weather those storms together.

Spiritual boundaries can be looked upon as being invisible yet formidable barriers that delineate or help us define our personal energy. That way, we don't spend unnecessary time and strength on those matters that don't add to our purpose.

Spiritual boundaries are designed to provide barriers that help protect us from things that can take us away from our purpose. They serve as a mechanism to better assist us in our overall well-being. Spiritual barriers are also designed to provide a safeguard in our inner being. They could possibly help us ward off unnecessary disruptive external mistakes and second guessing ourselves at every turn.

To grow into the very best version of ourselves we must allow ourselves the opportunities to know ourselves outside of what we think we should be or by comparing ourselves to others we deem better, stronger, wiser, or smarter than ourselves.

While every human being is different, being able to apply spiritual boundaries into our lives will afford us the ability to entrust those boundaries to provide an essential aspect to our new journey toward our personal spiritual growth and enlightenment.

Spiritual boundaries are a matter of setting aside as much time as needed. Through prayer and meditation, reflect upon what matters most to you and those you deeply care about and hold dear in your special circle.

They allow yourself to deepen the connection with those or the things that serve as the valued purpose of why you are here in the first place. Life was never meant to be lived in a bubble that only revolves around ourselves or me, myself, and I. Instead, it is meant to live out the very best version of ourselves and to make noticeable differences in the world that begin in our individual homes. Then, we spread them abroad or wherever our journeys may take us.

In today's society, my heart hurts for those parents who are really doing the very best they can with juggling so many balls in the air. They work hard, making every attempt to provide for their families. The last thing they need is to spend extra time on who is for them and who is not. They literally run from sunup to sundown, trying to make every event or sporting event their child is enrolled in. But at the same time, they are also stretching themselves thin and wearing themselves out so their children will never forget that they love them and want the very best for them—even when it comes with a very high price.

It is really no surprise that in our world today, everything is turned up to a higher expectation. Even then, there appears to be no rest for the weary. If you pattern your life by what is going on in the world today, you may very well never know who you are—always chasing the next big thing you think you need to stay innovative.

Day in and day out, I constantly see people chasing after things that have absolutely no heavenly value in the end. They add no value to their lives even now. At times we think, "If I can purchase a big house or new car or make a certain amount of money, our lives would be better for it." Perhaps it will temporarily. But like everything else, tomorrow will come, and the day will begin all over again.

Chapter Eight

It's so Hard to say Goodbye to Yesterday

I don't know about anyone else, but some things in life are quite difficult to say goodbye to—especially when those things matter so very much. You could never imagine your life being lived out differently.

Imagine, if you will, getting married in your 20s to the absolute love of your life and getting to spend the next 38 years filled with life, love, and adventure. Learning together, growing up together, and accepting and appreciating what each other brings to the table.

Throughout the years of growing together, you've learned how to respect, honor, and value the other's hopes, dreams, and aspirations. The support is there. The joy of spending time with each other watching football games, going to the movies, or going out to dinner is special. Sharing in the good times, the hard times, the challenging times, and even the disappointing times, you learn how to genuinely show up for the other no matter what. It takes a special person to do that.

How do you really say goodbye to someone who has always been the go-to person when you needed an honest sounding board? An old soul to share your heart with that didn't mind sharing your dreams, hopes, and aspirations?

You were so blessed, because you believed you had found your knight in shiny armor. He or she accepted you as you were and cared about every little detail of your life and interests.

How do you say goodbye to someone who made you laugh until your stomach hurt and couldn't stop smiling when you spent time together? Who always considered your emotions when you were not always right?

It is challenging at best to say goodbye to that person who loved you in and through all your mistakes, quick to forgive even when they were in the right. The one who loved being married and being the husband and the covering in the marriage.

What do you do when you wake up from the nightmare you prayed was only a terrible dream? One day you have to slowly accept and embrace that it wasn't a bad dream. And it is slowly becoming your new reality.

Not only is it a shock, but it is unbearable raw news you will have to allow yourself to face and accept over time. It's not only hurtful, painful, scary, and at times overwhelming but you feel with everything in you, "This cannot be my life."

At first, you know you are still breathing, but somehow, you could not seem to catch your breath. You feel as though the life you once had and thoroughly enjoyed would somehow find its way back to you. All would be forgiven and return to what you may think was normal. But that's not remotely the case. The harsh reality is nothing will ever be the same again. Your life you once held close to your heart has now been taken from you. Now you have to learn how to navigate anew.

This is the tricky part, because you know how to walk. But somehow, in the moment, you cannot feel your legs beneath allowing you to move.

You have so much you want to say in your head. However, the words won't formulate in your mouth, and all you seem to do is cry. No words, no sound—just tears and more tears. As if that will be for the next however long your new language that only the angels up above can interpret.

Day-by-day and moment-by-moment, you slowly embrace that life has thrown you a harsh, unfamiliar curve ball that left you numb and somewhat isolated from the heart down.

In the days, weeks, and even years, over time, you may be tempted to sit on the sidelines and watch all your old dreams and memories you once held tightly to pass you by.

You slowly accept that those friends you shared with other couples now shrink away under the auspice of they are too busy to call or hang out like you use to.

The real reality is that in time, we witness our lives through what could be deemed as our new normal change and evolve through our life circumstances. New situations become a real game changer. Those things dear to us can become hard for us to say goodbye to because we treasure them so much.

At some point during our new journeys, it will be difficult to accept the thought that those things we must say goodbye to now no longer serve us in the capacity they once did. Things like special events, birthdays, anniversaries, date nights, leaving special notes around the house or in the car. Last-minute getaways, vacations or just spending quality time together sharing and loving one another.

It's funny how you remember and reminisce about what once was in your mind silly, unnecessary, and perhaps unappreciated. But now, what you wouldn't give for that one more time to do it all over again.

Regardless of the loss—whether it was a job, income, home, vehicle, career, loved one, relationship, friendship, etc.—turning the corner is never easy. There seems to always be one last word or conversation we feel we should have had before walking away.

Losing a loved one that meant the entire world to you is not only heartbreaking but also extremely challenging to wrap your brain around. That individual is gone from your life forever, and all you are left with is a lifetime of memories to hold on to.

Think about this, you have been employed at a company for years. You have enjoyed the journey thus far. Not only have you worked for this particular employer for years, but you have also enjoyed the timeframe you have invested over the years. Without being aware of the shift happening in your life, one day, you are served notice that your reign with this company is coming to an end before you expected it to. Now, you feel blindsided and maybe betrayed.

You never dreamed of doing anything different from working at that company. Until that moment, you made a career out of your employment there. It is not just a job but a career and a part of your regular routine. You didn't have to think about your work tasks or your assignments or your various projects for the day. You could do them with your eyes closed. Over the years, you can remember the months and years you poured your blood, sweat, and tears into your daily workload. Now, you couldn't imagine anything different.

Here you are at this time in your life. You find yourself asking, "Why now in my life, just when I was looking forward to retirement? Why now, when I have so much to look forward to? I have lost it all. Why now? I feel so betrayed and abandoned.

"Are you telling me my life has come to this point, and this is all I have left to represent all I have been through? Is this where we really part ways? Am I just supposed to start all over again from this point in my life? At my age? In this season in my life?

"How am I supposed to move forward in a totally different direction for my life? God, I don't even see how this thing is going to work out for my good. I don't see how your plan is working out for my good and for your glory.

"Have you not considered I am struggling? I don't have the finances. I don't have the confidence. And I don't have the resources, the support, or the influences it takes to move me forward in life. God, I have more enemies than I have friends. Tell me! Just how am I supposed to succeed?"

Be still and wait for this small still voice that says, "Fear not, for I am with you; be not dismayed, for I am your God; I will strengthen you, I will help you, I will uphold you with my righteous right hand." (Isaiah 41:10 KJV).

At times, the pain and loneliness you feel inside can become unbearable and too much to handle or bear. There is no replacement or substitute for the missing piece of the puzzle that you lost. The missing piece no longer there was the original of its kind.

What we have to realize is that even though we don't understand what's happening, God knows our ending from the beginning, and He alone is prepared to see us through. Through what you may ask. Through it all. The good, the bad, the ugly, the misunderstanding, the hurts, and the pains. God is able to do...

When life knocks us to our knees. When we don't see it coming for us or we are left without direction or answers, it is imperative to know our God lifts up a standard before us to keep us safe.

In other words, our God will intervene in a mighty and powerful manner. He will intercede in a mighty way to deliver and protect His people in the face of an ominous threat or intense spiritual warfare.

Not only is our God our Way Maker, but He is also Able to make all our detours and crooked paths plain and straightforward.

He will not suffer our foot to be moved, because God, who is more than enough, guides and orders our path from the beginning until the end of this life. He makes sure we arrive on time and in time with His spoken promises over our lives.

We don't have to walk the floor at night, or tossing and turning in bed. Wringing our hands and sweating over the small things, the unimportant things, the bothersome things, the trivia things. Not those of us who put our trust and our faith in the Lord Jesus Christ—nor in His handiwork.

We have seen Him show up and show out on countless occasions. We have watched Him become the way where there wasn't previously a way. We know Him to be a wheel in the middle of a wheel. The One who is able to keep us in perfect peace if we work out His plan for our lives and simply follow the leading and leadership of His Mighty hand.

When we learn how to rely on the Word of God for our individual lives, we will learn how to stand on His Word, being fully persuaded that whatever God has spoken over our lives through His Holy Word will come to pass.

Even though in the natural or the flesh, there will be those things and times in our lives where it will difficult to walk away from what we are comfortable with. Those things we have gotten accustomed to or have been relying on, and we don't want to change or start over. We must remember our lives do not belong to us, but to God. We must learn how to follow His lead and not lean unto our own understanding.

When we learn how to trust God's process for our lives, then we can begin to see the sunshine coming through a very dark and dismal time in our lives. We can believe God is the same God in the dark as He is in the sunlight. That He will be the same strong tower when I was in trouble, disbelief, dismayed, and delayed as well as disabled. He is still the True and the Living God. He never changes. He always remains the same.

When I really get this belief and faith deep down in my soul and my heart, I can rest in God. I can look unto Him who I recognize as being the Author and the Finisher of my soul. I can walk through the valley of the shadow of death with an understanding that I must allow some things to die off, so I can begin anew with less baggage and debris.

The more I trust and rely upon God and allow myself to take His yoke upon me and learn about Him, the easier my burden of trying to make my own way will become. Now this is not to say I will no longer have life's challenges. It just means I won't have to travel alone, because He is with me.

The more I learn about my new walk in Christ, the lesser the pain and the various angsts will have a debilitating foothold over my life. The more I allow the Holy Spirit to reveal to me about my future with God, the easier it will become for me to let go of my past and the non-essentials that once kept me grounded and ill-effective in my daily walk.

It is important to know that as long as I am ignorant of God's goodness that lies ahead of me, the more fearful I am about letting go of those things that kept me bounded and beat up. I will forever keep looking at my mistakes, mishaps, and misgivings as if those were honorary badges to be worn proudly.

Absolutely not. We were built for more than that. In fact, we need to know that for those who trust in God, our greater days are ahead, not behind us. Our very best is yet to come. We need to shed any and everything that is not able to move forward with us off. We need to lay aside every weight that slows us down and run, not sashay, into our future.

We don't need to walk around it seven times and cry until the walls fall or at least remain propped up. We need to lay it all aside and run face forward into the unknown, trusting and believing God has blessings for those who believe with our individual names on every one.

Chapter Nine

Nurturing Your Garden

I WANT TO BEGIN this chapter by letting you know that by no means am I a gardener, nor would I consider myself to have any expertise of gardening. However, I grew up on a farm and watched my mother intently grow her garden in the summer. It was very intriguing.

Growing a garden is an art, and one must have an eye for details and patience to grow a plant to its truest form. My mother would often sing, hum, plant, and grow with joy.

Not only must a gardener have a green "anointed" thumb, but they also have to enjoy what they do. They must plant with intention and have an eye for grooming and pruning.

In Mother's garden, she planted everything with detail. She planted flowers, cabbage, collard greens, mustard, onions, corn, tomatoes, okra, etc. You name it, and she most likely planted it.

Not a day went by that she was not outside in her garden, nurturing it, watering it, and singing over her crops. She made sure she was careful to oversee her seed investment by any means necessary. If those pesty bugs and insects were planning to destroy her garden and her personal efforts to make her plants grow, they had to contend with her first. She somehow seemed to always win.

In another way, I can also use gardening as a metaphor for dealing with pain and heartache. In life, you may have planted one thing. But as your life develops, you often experience setbacks due to pesty and annoying delays, disturbances, and hinderances alike.

When that happens, and it will, keep living. You must continue to tend your garden by making sure you are careful to keep a watchful eye on your seed. Make sure you control and oversee what pesty thing is trying to enter in to destroy what you are trying to grow.

Just a word of warning, though. Look carefully to make sure you are not pulling up or destroying what could be beneficial to you during your growth process.

I learned a main element from watching my mom plant her garden. She was very selective in her choice of what she planted. She didn't just grab a handful of different seeds and throw them onto the ground without making sure the location she had chosen was in place and fitting for that seed to grow. Not only was the proper hole dug for that seed to be placed, but the correct spacing for the seed to expand was allowed or considered so the seed reaped its intended harvest.

Seeds, in this instance, is likened to a dream or a personal goal one has for himself or herself. While it is important to have a dream, it is equally important for that dream to be nurtured and carefully watched over. Nurturing yourself involves actively engaging in certain practices and demeanors that support and promote your overall health, wealth, well-being, and mindset for the happiness you want to receive.

Nurturing is not only a good idea, but it is of vital importance that you do so. Self-love must be at the head of your list and serve as a priority, but it must be taken seriously at all times to become the best version of yourself.

Sometimes, in our personal lives, we can become caught up in the cares of this world. We lose ourselves in the midst of it all and open ourselves up to the stressors swirling around us. This is why nurturing is so necessary to pay attention to. Nurturing is not only being mindful of how we take care of ourselves or the lack thereof, but understanding that nurturing encompasses caring for our physical, emotional, and psychological needs in a compassionate and intentional manner.

Although it sounds simple to do, let me assure you it is anything but. For some reason, the world has bought into the idea that the more things we sign up for and the more activities we have on our schedule means we are important. Our busy calendars suggest we are in high demand. Therefore, we do pretty much everything in our power to meet those demands whether they are beneficial or not.

Our personal nurturing should never be taken for granted, overlooked, or not taken seriously. When we choose to take time out to provide nurturing for ourselves, we will come to realize it is one of the most fulfilling components to our overall spiritual health.

No matter how busy our lives become, we must learn how to take time to intentionally nurture our spiritual well-being and create the space for positive things to flow and enter our life. That way, we become more fit and fortified for the journey we are about to enter.

Nurturing ourselves sets us up for success, not in terms of collecting more worldly materialistic things but those things essential to our purpose. When we make the time to do so, we become more resilient and non-judgmental of others when life gets difficult. Just by tweaking areas of our lives that are malnourished and unprotected, we can literally raise the quality of our lifestyles and make ourselves less susceptible to depression, oppression, anxiety, and stress when trying times come.

To become the best version of ourselves, we must put ourselves first but not in a selfish way. Daily, we should carve out time to practice healthy mindfulness—whether through meditation or just listening to a motivational message. There again, practicing mindfulness is not an easy thing to do. When we practice mindfulness, we deliberately and intentionally focus our attention on the present moment.

It means not allowing your mind to wander off to something else that only serves as a distraction from what is really important. Mindfulness is the art of being able to bring about a deep awareness and understanding of everything as it happens in real time.

Another great attribute to nurturing our garden is thinking about how and what we eat by deliberately practicing spiritually healthy ways we eat. Remember, like gardening, what we plant is exactly what we are going to reap as a harvest. Being keenly aware that what we put into our bodies is exactly what we are going to foster as the outcome. We must understand the divine connection between our mind, body, and soul in order to find the right balance for our lives.

Therefore, it is necessary for us to put time and attention into caring for our overall health as a major priority. If we want our bodies to function as they should, then it stands that we must be willing to do the necessary work it takes to foster that outcome.

When we make time to care for our bodies like we tend to a garden, we automatically create the appropriate space in our lives to provide the appropriate time to care for the health of our soul. If we chose not to make our lives and health a priority, then we must ask ourselves, who else is supposed to do it?

Being mindful of what we put into our bodies, or how we *feed* or *nourish* our body, is essential to this concept. Making every effort to put our overall health first can reflect how much more energy we can have and how much our mood can improve simply by eating whole, clean foods every day.

I realize that the older I get how extremely important it is to move our bodies daily. Whether we take a walk to the mailbox, walk around the block, or do some work in the yard or the garage, just move that body. Physical activity is another physical aspect that impacts overall, comprehensive health and wellness, *including* your spiritual health! And this doesn't mean you have to run marathons or climb Mount Everest. It just requires that you move your body.

Now, a lot of us don't want to invest in a gym membership or purchase a lot of workout equipment we already know we won't use like we need to. So we are very hesitant to do anything. But moving our bodies does not have to become a chore or a heartache. Moving our bodies could mean doing natural activities you enjoy. Taking a brisk walk, dancing, or chasing your kids around all count toward moving your body.

Nurturing our personal garden means planting those seeds that help us become stronger growers and defined nurturers. By getting out into nature, we get to look at sceneries we may have never witnessed before. We can find so many wonderful nuggets outdoors, because nature connects us to each other and to God. However, in today's society, we are often working inside for hours on end. By the time we finish working, it is almost dark or late into the evening.

As we live increasingly inside, it is estimated that Americans spend up to 90% of their time indoors. This has caused us to start losing the connection we once took so much pride in. No matter what, nature brings us a connection to a higher power and a pure sense of soulful being we cannot get sitting and staring at our computer screens all day.

I watched as my Mother tended to her garden. She got so much joy out of tending it daily. She made sure to keep the weeds, bugs, and even animals out of it. But another great joy from gardening Mother received was the gift of laughter and pure joy over her personal accomplishments.

Laughing is another one of those wonderful things for our health. In fact, laughter can relieve stress, relieve pain, and promote relaxation. But laughing can do more than that. Laughter can connect us to each other. Studies have found that most people are looking for humor in potential mates, and laughter is a sign of attraction. Additionally, laughing can bring us together. Because shared laughter, or laughter that happens by multiple people at the same time, can .

Another vital component to nurturing our gardens is practicing acts of kindness. A physical garden grows successfully by the love and the work put into its growth. That means it has to be watched over, tended to, and carefully handled.

As we continue to nurture our overall mental, physical, and spiritual garden, it is necessary to strive to practice Acts of Kindness. They create and strengthen our divine connection between living beings. Not only did my mother enjoy growing a personal garden, but she was also willing and eager to share her harvest with her sister and family as well as anyone else who she believed was in need.

As we continue to grow in our own spiritual garden and nurture the important things we need to grow, we can come to appreciate and value connection to one another. When that light-bulb moment happens, we come to understand that when we give more freely, we will treat each other with respect and integrity, and we can also trust one another.

Kindness is essential to unconditional love. It's the glue that helps connect us to each other and can help us feel fulfilled, meaningful, and peaceful on a spiritual level!

I believe my mother was in her element most while she tended to her garden. While out there, she looked as if being there provided her with an open space to be her authentic self. Like listening to music for some of us, being in her garden appeared to relax her.

True gardeners get joy out of watching what they planted grow. They realize the seed flourished because of their tending to it correctly as they applied the love and attention it needed to succeed.

So, it is when we truly connect with our friends and those individuals who we love and enjoy their company. When we learn to nourish our souls, we realize we find the things that help us with our connection to the incredible world around us, truly feeding the true, pure nature of our spirit. Connecting with other people can do just that.

Another very important aspect of nurturing our garden is taking the time to allow our seeds in the ground to germinate before we expect an enormous harvest. To nurture our minds, bodies, and spirits, we must get enough sleep. Sleep and deep rest can truly nurture our souls. This is more than just getting in a few minutes for a nap here and there. Sleep is essential for our physical and mental health. But sleep is necessary for our spiritual health too.

From a spiritual perspective, lack of sleep is a big way we block our power, creativity, and intuition. Sleep is the time when the body has a chance to repair. When our body can't repair itself, we not only feel ill, but we also feel blocked. Sleep is a great way to nurture our nervous system and boost our immune system as well.

Over the years, Mother became an expert in gardening. She was careful to know where to plant certain seeds, the spacing of the seeds, the lightening, and the timeframe in which to plant her seeds. She was in it to reap it.

Likewise, when nurturing our spiritual garden, we must put in the work and look for things that will spur on our spiritual growth. We must learn how to draw nearer to God so He can and will draw closer to us.

Drawing closer to God does not mean by my definition literally shuffling from one natural step over to Him but relinquishing all rights and authority over to him completely. It means surrendering my utmost will for His higher will and divine authority over my life.

It means trusting Him when the seeds I have planted in my garden do not seem to have taken root and there is no sign of growth in sight. I can still trust God immensely, because I know for myself He won't ever fail me.

Sometimes, in order to discover the deeper side of our relationship with God, we need a deeper look at our own spiritual growth through the lenses of how the Word of God speaks to us. Jeremiah 29:11 (NIV) says, "'For I know the plans I have for you,' declares the LORD, 'plans to prosper you and not to harm you, plans to give you hope and a future.'"

I am realizing that to be clear about those plans, so we can walk in rhythm and in alignment with the will and purpose of God, it is important to keep a journal or piece of paper nearby. Then, we can capture the thoughts or leading of the Holy Spirit when he whispers to us.

I wanted to share one final thing with you about nurturing our gardens. It is crucial to keep our gardens decluttered from all unwanted things that will stunt our growth and delay our true harvest.

Studies show a huge connection between the clutter we have weighing down our spirits and lives and the clutter we have in our physical space. Once we begin the process of decluttering, we can make open space that often leaves us feeling lighter and more confident and able to take on life as it comes.

Lastly, let's never forget to add a healthy dose of gratitude for our spiritual growth. Choose to thank God each day for the seeds He alone plants in our lives. Through our genuine faith, trust, and belief in Him, we grow. Practicing genuine gratitude in our everyday lives can routinely impact on our sense of well-being and balance. When we have alone time with God, we can take time to write down thoughts in our journal about the best things that add to our life's satisfaction.

Overall, when we choose to nourish our souls, it doesn't mean to force yourself into spiritual enlightenment. It's a slow, gradual process that can bring us greater satisfaction in our lives. There is no right way to nourish the soul. Hopefully, these kinds of activities can help us connect, find appreciation, relieve stress, and find a deeper level of peace in our lives.

Chapter Ten

Spiritual Eyes Wide Open

> *"The Spirit of the Lord is upon Me, because He anointed Me to preach the gospel to the poor. He has sent Me to proclaim release to the captives, and recovery of sight to the blind, to set free those who are oppressed."*
>
> Luke 4:18 (NASB)

IN MY VERY HUMBLE opinion, if there were ever a time for men's eyes to be open to the unadulterated truth, it is now. Throughout the Bible, there is reference to spiritual eyes as the ability to see beyond the physical realm and into the spiritual realm. This perception allows us to see God's unseen realities and understand His true will for our individual lives.

I am fully aware that if I am to lay hold to the precious gifts and blessings of God over my life, it is imperative that I follow hard after Christ and Him alone. Not only am I to be familiar with scriptures, but I must be obedient to their sayings and trust God for the outcome of it all.

The world I know appears to be starving for someone to make them famous, known, important, or great. To me, it is in that order, and they will do just about anything humanly possible to make that concept happen for their lives.

The mere thought of waiting or depending upon God is almost ancient if not laughed to scorn—sadly by both some believers and non-believers. Perhaps most of that is because we live in a world whereby our own doing, we can achieve these things in an "instant." Sometimes, literally overnight. The problem with that concept is that a house build upon sand alone will not and cannot last in and of itself. It needs support and must be anchored in something more concrete than head knowledge or a great idea in the works.

In the world today, it seems as though some people are obsessed with self-discovery as it relates to overnight sensation and instant success no matter the cost physically as well as financially. The idea of doing the appropriate hard work it takes to get there, along with due diligence and homework plus seeking God, is for the birds.

Opening our Spiritual Eyes and waiting on God's direction for our lives is not just a good idea. It is the only meaningful way to proceed. Having our Spiritual Eyes opened by God helps to connect with Him and His plan for our lives. When we allow our Spiritual Eyes to become opened by God, we come to the revelation that all around us, the spiritual realm exists. However, we cannot see it in the natural. In fact, it blinds us.

It is not enough just to be acquainted with God or to be familiar with His teachings. Outside of the scope of building a real relationship with Him, we must make our relationship with God a priority. We must desire to have a real encounter with Him. One that will stand the tests of time. No matter what is happening in our lives, we will come to know that God alone is able.

Building a real relationship with God is not a bunch of rules and regulations or dos and don'ts. It is our heartfelt hunger to establish a more meaningful and deep-seated relationship far beyond head knowledge.

When there is a real, intentional drive to learn more about our Spiritual Eyes being Wide Open, we are willing to learn the differences between spiritual eyes verses spiritual blindness. From this experience, we learn that to do so will be a game changer that will eventually transform the total trajectory of our walk in Christ.

Spiritual blindness is simply choosing not to believe there is a God and that Jesus Christ, or the gospel, could not possibly exist at all. The choice is to turn a blind eye to the possibility that either could exist or accept the mere fact that you can make it solely on your own.

Spiritual blindness can also cause individuals to think that somehow everything they possess or ever will possess has come about from their sheer ability to manifest it through hard work, luck, chance, or perhaps using a vision board.

In the book of 2 Corinthians 4:4, the gospel makes it very clear that the god of this age has blinded the minds of the unbelievers so they cannot see the light of the gospel. Therefore, it is most difficult for anyone without spiritual insightfulness to possibly understand how spiritual enlightenment works.

The danger in spiritual blindness is when non-believers don't feel appreciated, valued, or worthy, there is the tendency to pursue or receive spiritual gifts outside of the plans and direction God has for them to pursue. Most often, they will turn to other options of lesser value and will only bring about temporary happiness and excitement. When this mindset sets in, it is difficult for many people who don't accept the love and grace of Our Father to live in a place of frustration and defeat. Even when they have or experience bountiful success in their lives, they don't know God personally. And as human beings, we tend to fight what we don't understand or trust.

Admittedly, in the crazy society we live in today, it can be quite challenging to build a relationship with Christ. There are so many diverse versions of what true Christianity means.

More times than not, Christ is blamed for all negative disasters, evil hardships, and calamities in the world. On the other hand, more often than not, His name is rarely mentioned when we as a people are blessed.

This is why I believe it is imperative that we ask Jesus Christ to come into our hearts. According to the Book of John, Chapter 3 verses 3-7 (NLT), "Jesus replied, 'I tell you the truth, unless you are born again, you cannot see the Kingdom of God.'

"'What do you mean?' exclaimed Nicodemus. 'How can an old man go back into his mother's womb and be born again?'

"Jesus replied, 'I assure you; no one can enter the Kingdom of God without being born of water and the Spirit. Humans can reproduce only human life, but the Holy Spirit gives birth to spiritual life. So don't be surprised when I say, you must be born again.'"

It is imperative to understand that living in the world today, the enemy of this age will do any and everything within his limited power to make sure our natural eyes never become open to the truth of God and what He has for us. He personally prides himself on keeping mankind blind and deaf, as well as being spiritually asleep at the wheel of life.

When I think about Spiritual eyes, I see it as images in my mind's eye coming directly from God. When God shows me something from the past, present, or future, I can capture the revelation from it because He has provided me clarity to do so.

One of the most important factors I gleaned from this knowledge is that these mental images mean nothing until I have gained the spiritual understanding necessary to know I do not need to figure out the logical side. Why try to lean on my knowledge or idea of what I think? Instead, I can learn how to lean on and trust God by choosing to read and study His Word for myself. In that regard, I need to ask God to interpret the meaning of these images so I will be able to gain insight as to what He wants to show me through these impressions. When Jesus disciples us, our spiritual eyes will open to a whole new level of understanding.

I have learned not to simply seek God's guidance when I am in trouble or when I feel as though I have no other way out of my situation or circumstances. But I choose to seek Him, because I treasure His guidance in my everyday life.

Ephesians 1:18 references what some might think of as a curious phrase. "The eyes of your heart be enlightened." This means a spiritual understanding at a heart level. In this reference, it appears Paul was describing the heart seeing with eyes that have been divinely illuminated by God. One of the purposes God gives us spiritual eyes is so we can follow His will for our life and encourage others in the process.

Another important benefit of seeking the presence of God for my life is I have come to rely upon the Word of God to direct and order my steps. I am tired of making the same mistakes over and over again without any meaningful direction. When I seek the face of God and ask Him for His wisdom, I use my spiritual eyes to draw closer to Him in such a special and personal way. I become more aware of God's presence near me. It is truly interesting that the more I desire to draw closer to Him, I can literally feel His presence drawing closer to me. And it feels great!

Finally, always remember that when God is showing you things, ask for confirmation. When God confirms the images, you'll be more amazed and feel even more connected to Him. Never be afraid as you continue to read through the Bible. Don't be in a hurry to rush through the pages and peruse through the verses. But as you read, take the time to slow down, pause, close your eyes, and meditate upon what you are reading. In doing so, you will begin to see images appear in your mind that will reveal to you a whole new way of discovery.

Desire to praise and thank God at a deeper and intentional level than just saying the words you think heaven wants to hear. Worship and close your eyes. If any pictures enter in your head, ask God for an interpretation of what you have seen. It's okay to keep a journal to record the images and of the interpretation you have received. Also, it is perfectly reasonable to seek a believer who capable of using their spiritual eyes for greater insight and maturity in the matter.

Lastly, please remember that Spiritual growth is a process. It takes time, patience, and reflection. Sometimes God will open your spiritual eyes instantly, like Saul on the road to Damascus, or gradually. Jesus prayed for the blind man twice for him to see. Be patient. Spiritual sight will come.

If you are not necessarily comfortable praying out loud, or you don't know how to pray, you may feel more at ease with a prayer that goes something like this. "Lord, in Jesus' name, I ask my spiritual eyes and ears to open to hear Your Word and receive your visions. Father, thank you for opening my spiritual vision and for giving me Your Spirit of understanding and wisdom to interpret. I only want to see what you are doing. I pray this gift of spiritual eyes will help me know what my calling is. Thank You for pouring Your spirit on me so I can see images in my mind's eye, visions, dreams, and even heavenly angels. Please give me confirmations for everything you will show. Protect me from the enemy while I'm learning this gift."

In conclusion, never forget that God loves you and desires you to have this gift. You are worthy! God is always there to assist us in this journey to see with our spiritual eyes. He wants spiritual vision to be a part of our life so He can guide us through every day.

Chapter Eleven

God's Got a Blessing With my Name on It

IF YOU ARE STILL holding on to grudges for over five, ten, fifteen or even thirty years, you are not ready. If you still find it impossible to forgive others, although you really want God to forgive you, you are not ready.

If it still angers you to see others being blessed differently than yourself, you are still not ready. If you can't handle the way God chooses to bless someone else without asking your permission, you are definitely not ready to move forward.

Every Sunday morning during the meet and greet time at our church, this song is sung while the church fellowship happens. "God's got a Blessing (With Your Name on It!)" It's not only a popular song, but an exciting one as well.

Man, as long as the music is flowing and the praise team is harmonizing, and the air and the good heat is flowing in the services, people are smiling, hugging, and swaying along to the music, and interacting joyfully with one another. Unfortunately, when you are on your way back to your seat to sit down, if you glance quickly to your left and to your right, you can inevitably spot the face of that individual who has one of the most sour, uninviting looks that indicates, "Do not come any closer to me."

Not only are there cold looks, but you may also encounter the standoffish cold shoulder as well. You smile widely, hoping it will be received, but to no avail. You must remember you are still blessed, and God really does have a blessing with your name on it. You have got to learn how to walk on by on your way to God's greatness for you.

Perhaps, you are having to learn, like me, that because you enjoyed the song, you must take personal ownership. Hide the words in your heart and let nothing negative steal them from you.

It is a sad sight to see. The Word of God tells us "Blessed shalt thou be in the city, and blessed shalt thou be in the field." (Deuteronomy 28:3 KJV). Yet we struggle often to believe and receive those words for ourselves. We are anxious to be "blessed" and bummed when we have to suffer or wait for God's best. It is difficult for us to believe God's waiting time for us feels negative. And no one enjoys or celebrates what we think suffering represents.

Have you ever taken a moment to think about what it truly means to be blessed? Being blessed is not a lucky charm, or the luck of the draw, or getting everything we think will make us happy. Being blessed is coming to the understanding that God didn't have to be good to me, but He is. He didn't have to watch over my life and order my steps, but He does. He didn't have to keep me, even when I didn't realize He was truly keeping me from all hurt, harm, and danger. But He was. By the time I came into wisdom of understanding that it was His strong arm over my life, rather than my great ideas, I wholeheartedly believe and know. I am truly blessed.

As I look back over my younger and very naïve days when I truly didn't know any better, perhaps I had the wrong understanding of what being blessed really meant, too. Blessings should never be viewed as expected tokens or rewards given out for good behavior.

Nonetheless, no matter how you interpret blessings, the important thing is appreciation and thankfulness for understanding them, and acknowledging them with a grateful heart.

Being blessed can mean having good luck or fortune, experiencing a sense of well-being, or simply recognizing and appreciating the positive aspects of our lives. In short, blessings represent the abundance and positivity we experience—both materially and spiritually.

Interestingly enough, Christianity has its own interpretation of blessings, with them viewed as , grace, and kindness from God. The blessings are said to bring about spiritual growth and material blessings such as financial abundance and good health.

Regardless of the culture or religion, the idea of blessings is often associated with gratitude, appreciation, and positivity. To recognize one's blessings, it's essential to cultivate gratitude and have a thankful heart. By doing so, individuals can recognize the blessings they have, both material and spiritual, and appreciate them fully.

Along with blessings comes mature responsibility and accountability. Real blessings are not all about butterflies and tiptoeing through the tulips. Blessings are anything from breakthroughs to breakups, cups running over to being without. You see them, if you take the opportunity to investigate the meaning behind it.

Having a blessing with my name on it signifies I can have vast gratitude for everything God allows me to walk into. I am at peace knowing that whatever God has for me is not only for me, but it describes me. It becomes me. It is God's expressed plan for my life and my personal journey.

My blessed is detailed. It is carved out of God's nature for my life. It is unchangeable. It is indescribable to the naked eye. What may look like a disaster from the outside is actually deliverance on the inside. And it is causing me to see things from a whole different vantage point and to believe for more.

Sometimes blessings are things we would not ordinarily pick out for ourselves, because our description of blessing can be misguided and misconstrued. It can also be something we self-describe as being over the top, large exploits, public expressions, and grand entrances. The truth of the matter is our blessings can come in many shapes and forms. But they always trace back to one hand and from one means—the hand of God.

A blessing can also be looked at as a statement of good will and happiness said about another, along with the condition that fulfills those good words. I believe God's original design in creation was for His creatures, including mankind, to experience prosperity, peace, and fulfillment, but that design was ruined when sin entered the world.

Proclamations of blessing are a hope for God to restore His favor on our lives, as well as the lives of others, or a declaration of His inherent goodness toward us. However, the ultimate blessing God gave us is the new life and forgiveness that comes through faith in His Son, Jesus Christ.

The material blessings we enjoy from day-to-day are temporary. But the spiritual blessings available to us in Christ encompass time and eternity, as well as material and immaterial things. As the Psalmist said, "Blessed is he whose help is the God of Jacob, whose hope is in the LORD his God." (ESV).

Indeed, God does have a blessing with our name on it. And that blessing is to truly honor Him by accepting Jesus Christ into our lives as our Lord and Savior. Receiving and acknowledging Him in and over my life is everything.

Chapter Twelve

Trusting God With Your Future

Trust me, I had to learn, and am still evolving as we speak, because learning to trust God is just that. "Learning." Trusting God is not a one-hit wonder. Human beings will never be able to come to God in one setting and walk away from that moment totally informed and endowed with a lifetime of understanding, knowledge, and wisdom. In that case, we would never need to enter into his presence again. That's just not how it is going to work.

Trusting God is an essential element of true and saving faith that looks to God and finds peace, strength, contentment, and much more in Him, and all that He has done, is doing, and will do—both now and forever in His Son Jesus Christ.

It's a coming to the conclusion there is none other like God. He stands alone. We need His presence in and over our lives. There is absolutely nothing that can live and thrive and truly exist without His presence daily.

Trusting God is not meant to be an afterthought. It is definitely a must have. The very thought that I can navigate my daily life without His direction and guidance in my life is like trying to breathe without oxygen.

God is necessary for my personal life. But over the years, I have found I cannot make it without His presence leading, guiding, and teaching me the way. I cannot see myself trying to make decisions that will be beneficial or successful without His leadership.

When I am given the opportunity to minister to others, one of the main topics I leave with them is that we cannot be deceived in thinking or believing that we live on individual terms. Not only is that misleading, but it is wrong thinking. And it is inaccurate believing. If we need further proof of that statement, all we need do is turn around and look at the mistakes that could have been avoided had we asked God for discernment, wisdom, and foresight.

Instead of taking matters into our ill-informed and incapable, weakened hands, it is necessary at some point in our lives to conclude that no man is an island alone. We unequivocally perish without true knowledge that can only come by having a relationship with God.

When we walk blindly in our way, on our terms, and in our ideology, it is important to know we fail in the long run. It is not the will of God that we fail or walk around in the world with blinders on, simply hoping against hope that what we planned for ourselves is simply our choice. He doesn't want our lives to be thrown against the wall and hope that it sticks.

God desires everyone he created to have a long, fulfilled, and beautiful life. Not so we would all live comfortable, overjoyed, rich, and self-centered lives, but so we would look out for each other and genuinely lean and depend upon Him as the head of our lives.

I strongly believe we not only need to learn to trust God, but we desperately need to make it our number one mission in life to know Him on a personal and intimate level. When we make every effort to do so, we will find not only was this a good decision, but it is the greatest decision we could have made in our lifetime.

I am not recommending that we simply be introduced to God by way of visiting church or hearing his name called every now and then or when something terrible happens. No, it is much more than that. Learning to trust God means observing how trust relates to saving faith. Then we will trace how trust grows out of a knowledge of God, His promises, and His actions.

It is important to grow in our personal relationship with God by building a personalized relationship with Him through the reading of his Word and developing a private prayer life. Then allow the teachings of the Bible to change you by looking at biblical examples of trust and how it should manifest itself in our daily lives as Christians.

Until we come to the end of ourselves in thinking we know it all, we don't need help from anyone or anything. We are vulnerable and can fall prey to all types of mistakes and blunders. Because the truth of the matter is, we do not know it all. In fact, we are so far from it.

Sometimes we run across individuals who are confident they don't need a relationship with Christ. They can think for themselves, and they have all the education, ability, skills, and smarts to charter their way. Trusting God, they may think, is for someone else who is smart or sharp but on a lesser scale than others.

Nothing could be further from the truth. In fact, until trusting God becomes a priority for us this can become one of those truths we think we understand until we are called upon to do it, and then we discover that there is more to it than we realized. Trusting God is an aspect of saving faith which has been said to have three elements to it: knowledge, assent, and trust.

For a believer of Christ, we are commanded to trust God and to follow his commandments. Now, I know to some who may read this or who have ever heard this statement before; they may think of it as a curse, or a choke hold of some sort to do so.

The commandments are not miniature prisons sentencing or a curse; in fact, they are a blessing to those who are willing and humble enough to listen to and to accept that our way of doing things is nowhere near the correct way.

As followers of Christ, one of the most important things that must be understood about trusting God is that we are commanded to trust the Lord if we desire the good life. Not an easy life, but a good life.

While there are several references throughout the bible that lets us know that we are to place our trust in God, Proverbs 3:5-6 exhorts us to "Trust in the Lord with all your heart and do not lean on your own understanding.

If we are going to live a life of growth and progress in all areas of our lives, we must be willing to place our trust in God alone. The word of God encourages us to in all our ways acknowledge him and he will make straight our paths.

This scripture does not suggest that we trust God only in only good or successful times but at all times because only God really knows the plans that he has for us and if we want to please God, the Christian life is one of trust in God from the beginning to the end.

This walk of trust in the Lord also comes with belief, trust and faith. This faith, of which trust is a central component, is what distinguishes those who are in Christ from those who are in Adam, the federal head of fallen humanity (cf. Rom. 5:12-6:14).

I know that it can be quite daunting at times to place our trust in someone that the naked eye cannot see; however, everything about God is trustworthy because of who he is in the perfection of his being.

Our first inclination when it comes to trust is to place it in something or someone that we can see and interact with because to most seeing is believing. But we must remember that we are warned about trusting in men.

Not only that, but we are also warned about trusting in riches: "Whoever trusts in his riches will fall, but the righteous will flourish like a green leaf" Prov. 11:28 cf. Psa. 52:7; Jer. 48:7; 49:4. Rather than putting our trust in anything created, we are called to trust in the Lord our God, and for many good reasons.

God is not a creature but the uncreated, eternal creator. He is not bounded by time, and he will never cease to exist. Furthermore, he is not dependent on anyone or anything for his existence. He does not need anything because he is the source of life and breath and everything else Ac.17:25.

The Bible also teaches that God is also all-present, all-knowing, all-powerful; no one can thwart his will, resist him, and come out unscathed Job 9:12; Dan. 4:35. As the Psalmist says, "Our God is in the heavens, he does all that he pleases" 115:3 and the apostle Paul affirms that God, "works all things according to the counsel of his will" Eph. 1:11.

Without a doubt, trusting God is the only way to live especially when we are willing to place all of our faith and hope in him. God's sovereignty is absolute without in any way destroying or making irrelevant human freedom and responsibility. Nothing happens that he does not ordain. Nothing catches him by surprise. He knows the end from the beginning, and he will do all that he has purposed and bring his plan to completion for our good.

Please understand that knowing God as the sovereign of the universe we can trust him no matter what happens. We are safe in his hands. As Proverbs 21:30 assures us, "No wisdom, no understanding, no counsel can avail against the Lord."

We are completely safe in his hands. God is also holy, which not only means he is transcendent and glorious, but he is pure and without any sin or defilement whatsoever (Isa. 6:3; Rev. 4:8).[1] There is no evil in him and nothing about his love that is inconsistent with who he is as the righteous one.

Trusting God with our lives and our future is priceless. Nothing can undo what he has done and declared to be just for our lives Rom. 8:32-34.

God is also wise, which means that he knows the best goal and the best way to achieve that goal.[2]

It is critical to understand God's wisdom if we are to trust him.

Trust means this world, and our lives in it, represents a course charted by divine wisdom. God's wisdom is often difficult, if not

---

1. (Wellum)

2. (Grudem, 1994)

impossible, to see at this point in redemptive history, because we cannot see things from his perspective.

Another primary reason we can trust God with our future is the fact that God keeps His promises to us. God can also be trusted, because His Word is true, and He keeps all His promises. (See and .) The Lord pronounces a blessing on "the man who trusts in the Lord, whose trust is the Lord" (Jeremiah 17:7 ESV). He will be blessed because the Lord cannot lie, and He will keep all His promises.

Not only are these promises wonderful in themselves, but we can rely on them as God's word to us, the fulfillment of which will be more than we can ask or think (Ephesians 1:20) Our Lord has promised never to leave us or forsake us (Hebrews 13:5), to be with us always to the end of the age (Matthew 28:20).

At the end of the day, we can trust God for everything, because He has promised to keep us safe despite numerous enemies—both human and demonic—who want to destroy us. He is the good shepherd who cares for his sheep, and he tells us that no one can snatch us out of his or his Father's hand (John 10:28-29).

Equally important to know is that no weapon fashioned against us as the servants of the Lord shall succeed. We will refute every tongue that rises against us in judgment, because the Lord promised to vindicate us ().

What good news that is to know when we place our trust in God. This act of trust with God is not just now and then but constant. God is trustworthy, because he has acted in history to carry out His plan of salvation for His people.

Finally, by placing our trust in God for our future, we can depend on God coming through every time. I want to leave you with a few of the benefits we can count on receiving as born-again believers in Christ.

If we trust in God, we will obey him as our sovereign Lord, and because we believe He knows what is best. Disobedience and trust cannot coexist; if we trust God, we will walk in His ways and do what He tells us. Trusting God will help us wait on Him when He delays or is silent regarding our prayers or the fulfillment of His promises. If He delays, it is for a good reason. His actions are founded on His wisdom and love.

Let's not get in a hurry when trusting God. David writes in Psalm 37:34 (ESV), "Wait for the Lord and keep his way, and he will exalt you to inherit the land; you will look on when the wicked are cut off." We must do the same.

Trusting God will keep us from taking matters into our hands as if we know better than God what we should do. If we trust God, we will not be afraid. "Behold, God is my salvation; I will trust and will not be afraid; for the Lord God is my strength and my song, and he has become my salvation." (Isaiah 12:2 ESV).

When we trust God, we do not have to worry about fear. Fear comes when we take our eyes off God and start to look at our surroundings. In life and when we pass through the experience of death, we must cling to him. (Psalm 23).

If we trust God, we will be content with what He has given us. We know He promised to give good things to His people, and He holds nothing back (). He tells us to ask Him for our daily bread and to seek first His kingdom. We must believe He will supply our needs one day at a time according to his will ().

Those who trust God will act in faith. Knowing who God is, what He has promised, what He has done, and how His people have trusted Him in times of temptation, darkness, desertion, adversity, and affliction, as well as in times of joy and abundance, the Christian should be bold and courageous.

Chapter Thirteen

When God Whispers Your Name

EVEN IN INFANCY, a baby wants to hear his or her name called. Though they have not yet discovered their true identity, when they sense someone of authority calling them, they will either look up in amazement or in the general direction of the call itself.

With a soft smile or grin, I believe they are thinking, "Someone's calling me, and I must respond."

Have you ever noticed when a newborn first enters the world, one of the very first reactions that happens is that child cries. And the second is he or she will stare in amazement at the individual holding them. They don't even blink. They just stare as if they are trying to etched that image in their mind for future reference. Their little world is wonder. To a newborn, new beginnings are opening up to a whole new world compared to where they've come from after a period of nine months.

According to Goodparents.org, "Babies are more sensitive to sound than adults because they have smaller ear canals, which amplifies loud sounds even more...."[1]

---

1. (Are Baby Ears More Sensitive? A Parent's Guide to Sound, 2025)

As we continue to grow from infancy to a child and into our teenage years, we also enjoy hearing our name called in the form of acceptance, acknowledgment, and celebratory moments. No one likes to be overlooked, unseen, or unchosen for anything.

Years ago, my husband and I would talk extensively about being young and trying out for different sporting events. I tried out for cheerleading and he for football. Years later it was funny talking about it. However, back in the day, it was anything but. We discussed the embarrassment, shame, hurt, and the defeat we felt from not being chosen. In some instances, we were looked at and never given the slightest chance of being picked, much less given an opportunity to participate.

When you are a child, teenager, or even a young adult, these stigmas can follow you throughout your entire life if you allow them to take over your perception of who you believe you are. And no matter who successful you may be in your life, there may be times you revert to those places of old hurts and wounds of rejection. You may allow those moments to hound you for the rest of your life.

As we continue to grow from an infant to a child, into our teenage years, young adulthood, and even into our mature stages, we will never outgrow the need for validation, support, and yes, to some degree, approval from someone—especially those we hold important, dear, or as a mentor in our lives. At the end of the day, their thoughts, opinions, support, love, and feedback matter to us deeply. We value them. Depending upon who they are, what place they hold in our hearts, we care about what they think of us. And we hang onto every word of mentorship they provide to us.

I remember being around the age of five. One of my big brothers, Jake, lived in Michigan. He came home for Christmas and brought me a beautiful bright red bicycle with training wheels on it. Now what made it even more special, the handle bars had little streamers on them.

Even though I hadn't a clue how to ride the bicycle, to say that I was excited would be a gross understatement. I was grinning from ear to ear. I was so filled with happiness and joy that I remember springing up from the bed early that Christmas morning, hands lifted, showing all of my teeth, and screaming for joy.

Notice I had never ridden a bicycle in my very young life, and I had no idea how to ride one. But I didn't allow anything to stop me from trying. I jumped on it and gave it my all. Thankfully, Jake was there to help me figure it out as I went. After hugging him and screaming, he helped me get on and stood over me a couple of times to lead and guide me throughout the rooms with turning and balance until I got the hang of it.

Once I got the gist of how to ride, I let the hammer down, and boy, I went for what I knew. I was turning corners, running into doors, walls, tables, and unfortunately, people. I am happy to say today I feel assured that most of them forgave me for a toe nick or a running over that bad foot situation.

Need I digress, hearing my name called on that early, cold Christmas morning was like hearing the angels singing in my good ear. The call felt good, but even more important was that I heard the call, and it was not random or by mistake. The call was deliberate, distinct, and intentional.

The caller was calling my name and had me in mind for that very special moment. Today, you may ask me, "Brenda, what is so significant about a bright red bicycle umpteen years ago when you were merely a child who did not know how to ride?"

I am glad you asked. I would say, now, having lived a little and coming into a much greater understanding about the direction for my life, I would say three specific things: First, little did I know Jake's gift provided a way to explore and discover something new and challenging in my world. Secondly, I accepted the help and followed the instructions needed for me to enjoy and take full advantage of what the gift was given to me to do. Thirdly, through the acceptance of the gift, I look back at that special time spent with my big brother and the joy we both felt in that moment. Because he picked out this gift, took the time to put it together, and brought it to me said a lot about the giver himself. He did not merely hand me the gift. More importantly, he willingly invested in my growth and learning.

Many individuals do not necessarily like their names or to hear them being called out. Depending upon who is calling, there can be a strong possibility the individual may not respond to their name being called.

Nothing is more disrespectful than when my name is mispronounced and being spoken in a negative connotation. When this happens, don't expect for me to respond, react, or give it air time, because it is undeserved and unappreciated.

It's one thing for an individual experiencing difficulty with the pronunciation of a name. If that individual really wants to get the name correct, it is just a matter of asking for help. However, it is another thing when there is no genuine effort.

Names are very important, and yes, it is also necessary to pay attention to who is calling your name. Our names are important for various reasons.

Names describes a part of our life story and introduce us to the world. Our names serve as an introduction of who we are representing and what the world can expect from us. Each time our name is called, our name releases a tiny piece of our personal identity or DNA as an acknowledgment of who we are. It is a glimpse into the hidden purpose for our arrival.

Our names are not mere words which we simply "go by." But our names allow us to navigate our life story and tell others about the plan God has prepared for our journey. Even though we don't know the full reasoning for our being, the fun part is we do not have to make up the scripting as we go. Those who can learn to trust God with their life journey can follow along as He unfolds the manuscript at will.

Our names are inscribed everywhere. They are engraved on our birth certificates, driver's license, diplomas, degrees, certifications, plaques, marriage certificates, special announcements, baby showers as the parents, and even our death certificates. Our name matters.

Equally important is coming to understand the power of what our name carries. Once we grasp the power of our names and what that power is designed to do for us, perhaps we will change the way we introduce ourselves to others and the world. This understanding can help us take a second look at our purpose.

Names distinguish individuals in society. Our names represent the label which we answer or respond to. Our names are affiliated to our fingerprints and the distinctiveness of who we are within society. More than just a word, our name holds the story of our identity. It represents the cornerstone of our identity and connects us to our family lineage.

Our names represent our cultural heritage and hold personal meanings. They are the titles of our stories, and just like a well-chosen book title, our names can invite interest, curiosity, or affection.

Finally, our names can influence first impressions. Have you ever walked into a room and been introduced to a crowd or to others, and you hear, "Oh, so you're Brenda Murphy?" At first this may seem like a shock, or coincidence, but later, you will get a revelation or a sense that your name has been in the thoughts or the minds of others long before you arrived.

A name given by parents can profoundly express their aspirations and the virtues they wish to pass on. The first gift—a carefully chosen message parents send with their child into the world.

Still, there is nothing like hearing the Holy Spirit call your name. Honestly, nothing else comes remotely close to that feeling of being seen, heard, understood, cared for, or amazingly loved. Not like, not tolerated, not put up with, but loved for real.

God—the Most High God, the true and living God, no other like Him—God knows your name. He is in love with you and me. Not only does He love us to the moon and back, but He promises He will never leave us nor forsake us.

I don't know if you have given this much thought, but if there is ever anyone that you want to know your name and to hold it in the highest standard, it is the King of Kings and the Lord of Lords.

The Scripture signifies that when you hear your name being called, it's an indication God is well aware of you, yearns for your fellowship, and has a purpose carved out for your existence. Names are hugely significant to God. He has many names, and He changes people's names for the good.

Personally, when I really gained the revelation that someone who needs no one or nothing from me, truly knows my name and gave me His identity, it caused me to move from a place of merely existing to thriving and living in real time. When God calls our name, it is not just a basic general call. I believe it is a call of love, a call into fellowship, relationship, and commitment. It is a change for the betterment of humanity and for every individual.

When God calls our name, it is a unique call—a celebratory call and important call. This call means each person belongs to something greater than ourselves. This is a call no one should miss in life, because it is a true game changer.

I have always been interested in the fact that not only does God know my name, but He is genuinely interested in me as a human being. He is concerned about the things that are concerning to me and affect me. His desire for my life is to bless me and not to harm me. To protect me and to guide me through my life's journey, making sure that everything according to his will goes as planned.

I had to learn His plan is not always my desire to hear nor to follow. Sometimes we don't always see eye-to-eye about what I thought His plan should be for my life. Especially when life gets in the way and life as I want it to be gets rerouted into a totally different direction than what I have planned.

I am learning the difference between when someone is acquainted with me and when there is someone who truly "knows me." On the one hand, the person who is acquainted with me knows bits and pieces about me—perhaps those things they have observed, or I volunteered to share with them.

The mere fact that God needs no real introduction into my life, my space, my thoughts is an entirely different level of understanding. I ask myself from time-to-time, "Why would a God who already has a clear and precise knowledge of me want to be Lord over my life?"

What in the world could I possibly offer him? I have nothing to give. Nothing to add. Nothing to bring to him accept myself—flaws, weaknesses, imperfections, insecurities, and at times, my doubts. Yet the call from Him stands. The invitation is still on the table. Daily he waits patiently for me to respond and come to Him so I get to know Him intimately.

I must admit that while I am nervous, unsure, and at times a bit overwhelmed by such an invitation, if I am honest, I am also very intrigued and eager to find out more. That inquisitiveness drives me closer to Him. I want to know Him more and more. I am smitten by His love and affection for me. When I am in His presence, I no longer feel the outside forces that try to weigh me down or tell me I am not good enough.

There is something about being in His presence that calls me into the deep far beyond my norm and over and above my weaknesses and limitations. When I am in His presence, I do not see, think, or feel the same. It is as though time stops and stands still. I am truly in awe of Him. I know this will probably sound strange, but life as I know it in the natural world shifts for me. And I am in a moment of true transparency within His presence.

I feel that I am enough. I can see my life from a fresh perspective that I am everything He has made possible for me. I am not limited by time and constraints that often hinder my progress and hold me bound to unnecessary cares of this world. Not only do I feel free, but I feel glimpses of liberty to simply "be" who I am created to be. In the time I spend in God's presence, the old shackles that once held me hostage in my space of limitedness are no longer there. I feel as though I have been granted spiritual permission to roam and explore God's best for me.

I am fully persuaded through my personal time spent in the presence of God that not only does He know me, but when God whispers my name, He has only me in mind. That's our special time we spend together. That is our shared space of intimacy only the two of us share.

One of my favorite scriptures in the Bible is Psalm 91:1-2 (NIV), where it says, "Whoever dwells in the shelter of the Most High will rest in the shadow of the Almighty. I will say of the Lord, 'He is my refuge and my fortress, my God, in whom I trust.'"

Reading those verses always makes me smile, because I walk away feeling protected, guarded, watched over, and kept by the very best security. Talk about having access to being sheltered in place. That's it for me.

Being in the shelter of the Almighty God is beyond mindboggling. It's over the top, excessive, more than enough. Knowing this makes me feel safe, at peace and comforted no matter what is happening around me. Through His Word, God lets me know I have a safe space in Him where I can not only go but remain.

I understand life gets tough and rough from time-to-time. I am fully aware that the more I love and seek Him, not everyone is going to like it and accept me. Still, when I think about the fact that God alone whispers my name, nothing else on this earth matters to me, because the call is everything.

Daily, I witness his call on my life. There is something special about the way He introduces Himself to me. How He keeps on making special, unique, and specific ways for me out of impossible ways. The way He calls my name makes me smile like a school girl.

There is something about the way He makes Himself known to me.

Chapter Fourteen

The Next Chapter

MY SPOUSE AND I were married for 38 beautiful years. During those years we experienced life, love, challenges, heartache, pain, triumph, setbacks, setups, and everything in between. But God.

No matter what lied ahead for the both of us, I never wanted to do life without him. In my heart and soul, he was the necessary part of my life. He added flavor, solace, drive, and importance to my journey.

Audie was genuine. Funny. Thought provoking. Generous. Forgiving and caring amongst other things. He had a big loving and compassionate heart that always looked out for others. It didn't matter whether he knew them or not. If he could help others, he could be found doing so, no matter what.

During our beautiful years together, on so many occasions, I remember countless special things he did for me, but one in particular. He always had an uncanny way of making me laugh. Not just smiling, but truly laughing as if nothing else in the moment mattered.

He didn't hold grudges and was always very quick to forgive and move on. He absolutely chose to live his life in the moment and savored everything and everyone he deemed special to him.

Beyond the last 38 years, it goes without saying, he will always remain the absolute love of my life, my best friend, and the world's most amazing husband on this side of heaven. I will miss him terribly but will never forget him, because he will forever live in my heart and my memories.

I will be honest. The very thought of living my earthly life without Audie will take me time, acceptance, and effort. It will take deliberate intention and a genuine process. I give myself the necessary time, permission, and the will to move forward on my earthly terms. I will not be rushed, prodded, or told when and how to move forward—especially from those who have no dog in this personal fight.

The next chapter is not about speed reading through life. Quite the opposite—slowing down, taking slow, deep breaths, and absorbing my new normal on all fronts. I cannot deny this chapter in my life is very personal, scary, new, unchartered, and at times lonely. Even in these new waters and territories, I still want to embrace and tackle each emotion head on.

Daily I choose not to look for answers outside of who I am. I certainly do not look for others to supply me with what they may deem best for me. No matter if the exact same thing happened to someone else, each journey, pain, hurt, and devastation is different for each one.

Like everyone else, I never thought my life would end up in this chapter. At the outset of our married life, I never thought much about this particular chapter being sooner rather than later. I don't know anyone who can honestly be prepared for it.

I am learning for sure that before I can remotely plan to move forward with this new stage in my life, it is imperative that I am clear about the positive direction I want my life to go in. Making this transition in my life successful will require closure of the current chapter with realistic expectations and genuine and godly support.

Currently, I choose to think of my life as being a new chapter with different moving, excitable, and interchangeable parts. I imagine my new normal will be likened to moving from the end of one chapter to the beginning of another which will come with its own challenges, twists, and turns. Even still, I am encouraged to move forward one minute at a time with the Lord at the helm. The first step to accept is acknowledging that my new normal will be just that—new. I have to learn to embrace the newness that awaits me.

I am accepting that as I continue to grow, my personal life situation will change as the next exciting chapter enters. I choose not to be fearful and dread the next chapter but rather look forward to what the Lord has in store for me.

> *"For I am about to do something new. See, I have already begun! Do you not see it? I will make a pathway through the wilderness. I will create rivers in the dry wasteland."*
> (Isaiah 43:19 NLT)

It is important to me not to stay focused too intently upon the current door that has been closed. By doing so, I recognize that my emotions will hold me hostage to my pain, sorrow, loss, and regrets if I have any. Being respectful of that closed door can also assist me in not missing the new door that has now been opened and trusting God to what now lies ahead of me.

This scripture in Isaiah is important to me, because it allows me to expect great and exciting things for my future. Not only is it exciting to notice the new door as being opened, but to be excited about it.

Now, I must get myself in the posture of getting ready for my next chapter to begin. I am preparing myself for expecting good, better, and greater things to come into my life's journey. I am eager to live by the words of Jeremiah 29:11 (NIV) that say, "'For I know the plans I have for you,' declares the LORD, 'plans to prosper you {Brenda Murphy} and not to harm you, plans to give you hope and a future.'"

While everybody goes through big changes sooner or later, everyone has to face a new chapter in life. However, as we grow and allow ourselves to continue tunneling through the hard days and moments, we grow and watch ourselves evolve as our next chapter begins!

Admittedly, I am nervous but intrigued at the same time. I recognize how beautiful new chapters can be with time. Beginning a new chapter will take small and meticulous steps along the way.

Starting a new chapter for my life can either be self-guided or it can be due to allowing outside influences to affect my circumstances. The final decision can be left up to me. Or I can choose to open the next chapter of my life with guesswork and be thrown into it blindly without any earthly idea of where I may land.

I am looking forward to when the time is right to embrace the beginning of my new Chapter in Life. As I sit in my quiet place of choice, I welcome that sometimes life situations that push us to begin anew, ready or not, are the necessary chapters we need to read and accept—if we only accept them as positive. Of course, not while the hurts are still fresh and traumatic. However, in time, we have the option to choose how to start a new chapter in our life that can only come alive as we accept the challenge.

Beginning a new chapter in my life must be done gracefully and intentionally. It is important that I live in the moment while building my new chapter. How I handle my life with big changes and new windows opening for me is going to be essential to my happiness, mindset, and growth. Beginning the next chapter in my life will be handled with grace, success, and positivity. I have to be willing to let go of the past as I know it and embrace the willingness to move forward anew.

My previous life was everything I enjoyed, embraced, and held dear to my heart. Still, I understand it will be impossible for me to grow if I cannot let go of everything that could potentially hold me back and away from what God has for me going forward.

I will not pretend this new chapter will be easy for me to embrace. I am sure there will be times when special moments like our anniversaries, birthdays, first of everything will be exceptionally difficult to wrap my emotions around. However, this is why I am choosing to take all the necessary time to work through, not get by, my emotions of the past events before attempting to let it all go.

One of the hardest parts of the old chapter is visualizing my next chapter without the husband I loved and adored. The true friend I shared my entire adult life with. The one person I always knew I could count on for better or for worse. That vision of him by my side no longer exists. Now, it's just me.

Now, I have to visualize my entire world without him in it. I must visualize this next chapter alone. Slowly but surely, I am looking at my next chapter through fresh lenses. I am allowing myself to put into place some new ideas and hopes of what that looks like in real time.

Because I like to write things down as I visualize, this real chapter is no different. Once I have a clearer image of what I am hoping for, I am more than likely to achieve it.

One of my favorite ways of doing this is through my personal notebook. I am a visionary from my heart, and I have always been a dreamer. I enjoy combining my personal goal setting, visualization, and artistic creativity to make my hopes and dreams come alive. It only makes sense for me to stop and evaluate where I am now in my life. I must be realistic about everything—the good, bad, and the indifferent. Before I can move forward, it is imperative that I count and consider the cost of my next chapter.

This new chapter will include taking a good hard look at everything pertaining to my life. My habits, routines, mindset, health, and my entire well-being. I cannot be ignorant that these new changes will require some real adjustments. I personally know all too well that new beginnings in my life, along with new phases of my life, will cause me to make important shifts and adaptations.

I am not naïve in thinking my new norm life changes can be scary and at times very difficult. But I believe God is for me, and He is also with me on my journey. He will not steer me wrong.

I choose to believe and trust God now more than ever in my life. Through His leadership, the new doors He is opening before me will allow great opportunities for my growth, personal development, and self-discoveries.

Some of the first things I am going to work on in my new chapter will be identifying and getting rid of things that "used" to work for me but I cannot carry or allow in my new chapter. I am going to start prioritizing my overall mental and physical well-being by putting myself first. I am going to make more time by putting my self-care at the top of my list.

I will evaluate personal relationships and foster healthier ones. I am already creating a better sleep schedule and creating different money and savings plans. I will use my new planner to manifest my new chapter.

From day one, I will begin with positive affirmations, create invigorating and healthy routines, incorporate new hobbies that make me happy and alive, schedule more alone time as well as remind myself of my daily personal goals.

Starting out with these small but necessary tips is what I believe will make a world of difference within my new next chapter and improve my day-to-day life.

One day, I was watching an episode from Creflo Dollar. Toward the end of his ministry program he said, "Change your mind, change your living!" That moment spoke to me more profoundly, and it stays with me to this day.

Looking at this new chapter in my life will be an opportunity rather than an overwhelming change that will serve me as an essential pivotal moment in my new life. As I accept and embrace my new chapter, I will view it as being a perfect environment for my growth and self-improvement.

Equally important is the need to find a tribe, network, or circle of genuine friends that will support and not merely tolerate me into my next. Friends that will pray for me rather than prey on me. Friends that will be here for me rather than run out on me when the times appear tougher. I know this will be a change, but I place it all in the capable, blessed hands of God. I am fully aware He alone is able to see me through it.

I am so very thankful I have a praying support system in my family and a small circle of true friends to lean on. I know beyond a shadow of doubt that when I need someone to share my heart with or when times becomes difficult, I can rely on them.

One of my future sources of joy will come from my new Podcast called *Next Chapter*! I am so excited to start it and am working on that door being opened. This source of joy will be unique to each individual guest on my show. Personally, I enjoy pouring into others and helping them see that they, too, are very special and can live their best life.

Prioritizing my time is number one for me. I cannot afford to allow mental capacity for things that simply steal my time and waste my joy. When I look back over the years, I see too many opportunities when I gave away too much of myself to individuals who did not deserve it. They took advantage of me, robbed me of my kindness, and mishandled my generosity. However, today is a new day, and I am glad about it.

Today, I am all about proper self-care. Whether it is a new chapter or a continuation of the old one, self-care is pertinent. It is private, personal, and well overdue.

Beginning a new chapter in my new life is going to be a beautiful thing. I am going to embrace it. Welcome it and I will appreciate it.

Through Jesus Christ, I plan to stick with it. Stay strong in it. Lean on my personal support systems. Remain positive. And enjoy the journey.

Chapter Fifteen

It Gets Greater Later

WHEN I THINK ABOUT greater is coming, I am often reminded that my personal life gets better with my continual growth in God. When I immerse myself in His will, I not only believe I am on the right track, but I feel closer to Him in wisdom and understanding. I know He really does love me and wants nothing but the very best for me.

I have lived life long enough to come to the conclusion for myself that my life gets better the more I learn to trust the path God has ordained for me. The more I lean on and trust in the Word of God, the more I can release my faith for life's journey and become more confident that I will be just fine along the way.

I am so very grateful my life has led me into and around some very interesting points. But at the end of the day, I would not trade all of my experiences. To date, they have caused me to become sharper and more determined than ever.

For instance, I gain more insight into the will of God for my life by studying the Word, spending ample time in the presence of God, and listening to what the Holy Spirit is speaking to my heart. I recognize that as I step out on what I believe God is saying to me, I am benefitted by developing a stronger and unshakeable faith through the evidence of the manifestation of what I have received.

Understanding that my life gets greater later is not a cross my fingers and a bunch of wishful thinking. Rather, I choose to comply with a willingness to align my walk in Christ through the assigned plan He has put in place for me to follow.

The more secure I become in my everyday walk in Christ through gaining wisdom and understanding of His Word, I realize the importance of building a connectedness with like-minded other believers. My walk in Christ was never designed for me to walk alone.

To receive and accept that my greater is coming means I have to become open-minded to the things strategically placed in my path to walk through and out. Now, this does not mean this path or plan is going to be easy. That's okay, because it is God's plan for my life—not my made-up agenda.

My greater can only come through the goodness and the favor of God. I do not live my life by luck or lucky charms or any other gadget out in the atmosphere. Nothing good just happens and certainly will not last in and of itself without God.

Sure, I can start a thing. However, I cannot sustain that same thing for very long. I need discipline, guidance, insight, wisdom, and assurance along the way. Not only is it important for me to seek the help and guidance of God, but I must willingly step into that plan with complete trust and obedience along the way.

Greater comes in my life as I continue to grow in the knowledge and understanding of God's Word for my life. I can rest in His divine protection and preservation for my life as I continue to move forward and see the plan He has for me unfold right before my very eyes.

When I think about God having a blessing with my name on it, I come to the conclusion it is not always about planes and automobiles that make it a blessing but appreciating and being thankful for it all. My life, health, and my strength is a great place to start. When I think about blessings for me, I personally reference them as small gems wrapped up in miracles that assist me in discovering and developing my spiritual gifts while finding and fulfilling my purpose.

As I continue to walk in this revelation, I have noticed a considerable growth spurt in my increased joy, peace, strength, compassion, and love for myself and others. I am totally convinced I could never achieve this feat on my own. Believe me, I have tried and failed on many occasions.

The more I think about that song, "God's Got a Blessing With my Name on It" by Norman Hutchins, I am reminded of Proverbs 10:22 (KJV). "The blessing of the Lord, it maketh rich."

It reminds me that riches are from the Lord, and they should never be acknowledged or associated with anything else. Our blessings should never be attributed to the industry, diligence, insight, and merit of men. Our blessings can also be grasped as being made rich in a spiritual sense. The scripture alone describes the attributes of God and His blessing.

Now to be fair, we must continue the verse by looking at the last portion of what it says. The Bible declares in Proverb 10:22 that the blessing of the Lord makes someone rich. Not only that, but it also adds "no sorrow" with it.

How is that possible? Well, this verse lets us know there is a "rich" which can be attained by other methods that can sometimes bring sorrow with it—especially if it is not done honestly or with the wrong intention.

The Bible is clear that the Lord wants to bless us richly. Still, these riches are to come through the blessing of the Lord, not through deceitful works or anything which would not honor God!

Look at 2 Corinthians 9:11 (ESV). "You will be enriched in every way to be generous in every way, which through us will produce thanksgiving to God." This verse encourages us that God desires the very best for us at all times. He desires for us to be rich in all things. As we become rich in all things, we can be rich and generous toward others in every way—not only in our finances, but in every way! God does have blessings with our names on them.

All we need to do is lean on, rely on God and trust His processes for our life and never compare or compete with another individual about what God only has for you. Get excited!

Chapter Sixteen

Strategic Planning

As I watched thoughtfully, the end of 2024 faded out and the dawning of 2025 entered. I found myself feeling a little bittersweet. The thought that my incredible spouse and I would no longer be able to share this incredible moment together. To no longer look forward to sharing our new year dreams and hopes together left me a little sad at times.

Moving forward without the one you loved and held dear by your side for decades is not by any means easy. In fact, it can be challenging day by day. My only resolve for strength to do so is by relying solely upon Jesus to be my total refuge and my personal strength, every day, every minute, and every second of that day.

Interestingly enough, I can remember growing up and listening to "What a Friend we Have in Jesus" sung by my mom and other Christians I admired and even looked up to. Wow! I cannot tell you just how much that song has ministered to me in times of hurt, loss, and loneliness. When I think about the words to this song, my heart always ends up flooding over with emotions I didn't realize I had within me.

Death is real. The aftermath of the death of a loved one is very personal. It is very surreal. Processing the emotions that come during and afterward takes careful and intentional navigation.

I am finding in the road that lies ahead, one has to make sure every decision made should never be done without lots and lots of prayer and resting in God. Nothing should be rushed into for any reason.

Some days, life will look as though you can absolutely conquer the entire world hands down. Then there will be other days and moments you may not even want to climb out of bed, because you are not absolutely sure you want to do that right now.

Moving forward should not be a step approached lightly or quickly. Personally, I find myself praying more and moving forward less without confirmation from the Holy Spirit to do so.

Until June 5, 2024, I was so accustomed to making decisions with my spouse, us praying over those decisions and coming into agreement about the best route to take. At times now, it has been a bit overwhelming to decide anything without him. In those times, I seek the direction from God. I ask him to please lead and guide me in the right direction to go. In that prayer, I always close it with "Now God, if you are not talking, I am not moving without You."

Lately, I have found personal comfort in Psalm 121:1-8. This passage of scripture seems to comfort me in the days when I am conflicted in my emotions.

There are moments when I feel as though Audie is literally standing right next to me or riding in the car with me. I look over, and of course he isn't there, but his presence feels so real it forces me to look, anyway.

Whenever I think about him and us and what we once shared, tears flood my soul. A warm smile comes in like the ray of sunshine I see throughout the day that lets me know one day, the sun will shine again in my earthly life. And I will be able to continue tunneling through.

In Psalm121:1-8, the question is asked if my help comes from the mountains or from the Lord who made heaven and the earth! I have noticed when I pray now, I feel the closeness of the Lord has shifted in my life. I sense him being extremely near me in ways greater than before. Because of this closeness I sense, I am comforted that He hears me and is taking care of me in a manner I was previously unaware of.

Daily I place my hopes and dreams into His capable hands. I lay them intentionally at His feet, and I wait for Him. I trust Him, and I adore our time spent together. I need Him and am learning how to rest in Him.

Psalm 121:3 says He will not let me stumble. He himself will watch over me, and He alone stands beside me as my very own personal protective shade.

I am so very thankful in knowing it is the Lord who tells me the sun will not harm me by day nor the moon by night. It is Him that will keep me from all harm.

That's what blessed me—knowing and believing it is Lord Almighty who will continue to watch over my life daily as I come and go, both now and forever!

Talk about strategic planning. It doesn't get any better than that. I don't have to figure out what I should do and how I am going to make it. I don't have to struggle with trying to figure out what's best for me and how I am going to make things work for me. God already has those plans worked out.

I accept that the plans God has meted out for my walk in life were uniquely planned over 2,000 years ago. They are intentionally planned and detailed to my journey in life. Even when I am nervous about the unknown, God has assured me I will arrive on time, and I will accomplish all he has set before me—as long as I remain humble and obedient in His will.

Quietly, I pray to the Lord and allow it to be used for Kingdom building. I want the reminder of my days to bring glory to what matters most to Him. My heart's desire has always been to make God smile in all I do.

In the days, weeks, months, and years ahead of me, I ask Him to please open up those doors and illuminate the paths that are right for me. I want Him to heal my every hurt, wounds, and brokenness. I ask Him to shelter me in the midst of every storm. I want my life to align strategically with His will for me. I want to be planted directly in the place He wants me to be.

I recognized that often the plans I want for myself may not look like the place God has in mind for me. When this take place, it is me who has to decrease so the plans God has for me must take precedence. This can be nerve racking, because I don't know, nor am I informed about, all the details outlined in those plans. The interesting thing about it is I don't care. There is such a deep call within me that constantly encourages me to move forward and leave all the details up to God.

As I think back over my life, I can remember being the person who had to always know the details first before moving forward. I had to feel I could handle what was ahead of me before I signed off on it. I did not like surprises, and I wanted to remain in control.

But now I am finding out God works in my life the polar opposite of what I want. He calls, then He qualifies. He sends, and then He equips while I am on an obedient route. In other words, my trust in Him must be always at the forefront before His plan is revealed.

If I had to described what I believe is my outlook on the phrase "Strategic Planning," it would be do not make any plans for my life. Rest in the fact that God's plan is far greater than anything I could plan for my life.

I am also encouraging myself every day to believe the glass of my life is graciously half full rather than believing the glass is half empty. Since the glass is half full, it tells me I still have lots of room to grow, to learn, and to be thankful.

Chapter Seventeen

Setting the Stage for Success

"For as he thinketh in his heart, so is he: Eat and drink, saith he to thee; but his heart is not with thee."
                                                    Proverbs 23:7 KJV

IT REALLY GOES WITHOUT saying, if you want to be successful at anything you must do at least two things. One, prepare yourself for it. Two, do the work it takes to make it happen and sustain it.

Believe it or not, sustainable and authentic success will never come by wishful thinking or trying to naturally manifest it through vision boards alone. There must be work, diligence, faith, prayer, and direction to say the least.

We cannot simply pray about it, and somehow the heavens will open up, and the blessings come raining down upon us by manifold heaps. While we sing the song "God has a Blessing With our Names on it," we don't exactly know where those blessings are or exactly where to locate them in our own might. We must do personal work, no matter how long that may take. There is no point in hating someone else who may be or appear to be very successful, while we are simply sitting around looking long-eyed or jealous of them.

Real success is defined differently for each of us. It is not automatic symbolism. Even if an individual comes from a rich family heritage, everyone is expected to make his or her own way in life. Sure, the pedigree matters and can certainly cause many open doors so the journey will be much easier. Nevertheless, the effort must be sustained over time by its own integrity or the lack thereof.

Setting the stage for success is not directed toward one particular area in life. No, it is far broader than that. In the natural, success for some individuals is amassing large amounts of cash flow, mansions, lots of luxury cars, jewelry, real estate, and businesses, etc. However, we have seen time and time again, in the end, all of these "things" are merely temporary.

While having material things in and of themselves is not sinful, they should be items that you have as an individual rather than you being the owner of them. For some, materialistic things are the master of them. In a crisis, they are unable to separate themselves, fearing those things are all they have in life. If they part with them, they will declare they are nothing and have nothing.

The Bible is clear when it states, "For as he thinketh in his heart, so is he." (Proverbs 23:7 KJV). The sum of a man is what he thinks about and focuses on. Have you ever wondered how powerful and formidable our thoughts really are? Proverbs 23:7 suggests our inner thoughts shape who we become.

Our minds and our hearts guide our actions. It has been proven that when we feel happy, we smile more, our reactions are gleeful, our tone is positive, and our posture is welcoming and inviting. When we are sad or angry, there is an aridness about our total outlook. We do not want to around others, we are self-absorbed and sometimes even condescending and negative. Not only can our inner thoughts shape and influence are actions, be it negatively or positively, but it allows others to see them as well—no matter how hard to try to hide them.

It is also said that at the root or core of the meaning of this verse is one of hypocrisy. Meaning we may say one thing with our mouths. However, in our hearts, we don't mean it at all. It can be compared to the unethical salesperson who will tell you how wonderful you look in that outfit only to make the sale and score the commission associated with that sale. The bottom line, and the moral to this concept, is God hates hypocrisy.

I challenge us to consider three specific things prior to rendering ourselves to setting the stage for success from a broader spectrum. As we consider Proverbs 23:7 in its authenticity for our personal lives, we want to look at how we might respond to these three questions.

Personally, I associate authentic success that begins and ends with my intimate relationship with God. In Isaiah 29:13 (NIV), the scripture states, "The Lord says, 'These people come near me with their mouth and honor me with their lips, but their hearts are far from me. Their worship of me is based on merely human rules they have been taught.'"

I have learned over the years of my relationship growing in Christ, I am absolutely nothing without Christ at the helm of my life, leading, guiding, directing, and instructing me in the way I should go. Over the years, I have certainly made plans and orchestrated them my way only to end up buffering round and around in small, uneventful circles and becoming frustrated at best.

It has definitely taken me a while. But I have learned the hard way there is no real, honorable, longevity as it relates to success without Christ directing our paths. Not only do we see this mistake in the natural but also in the spiritual.

In churches everywhere, people give God praise from their lips or tradition, but their hearts are nowhere near him. They enjoy the idea of going to church and being in the atmosphere of what a church feeling may offer. Yet at the end of that service, they often leave with the same mindset they entered with prior to the service. They get caught up in the expressions of worship and forget it's the heart of worship that really matters. That's why Jesus said in (NIV), "Yet a time is coming and has now come when the true worshipers will worship the Father in the Spirit and in truth, for they are the kind of worshipers the Father seeks."

Be careful that your worship doesn't just fall in line with what everyone else is doing. Make sure you are worshipping from a sincere place, a true heart. A heart that desires God when you are in the service and more importantly, when you are not. This is what God desires.

Over the years, I have noticed how I listen to gospel music and not only how I listen to the music but the actual lyrics of the song itself. Prior to really paying special attention to the wording of the song, I was somewhat caught in the beat of the music itself. And just like most people, the beat of the music made it that much easier to sway and clap my hands while enjoying the song itself.

However, as I continue to grow in Christ, I have noticed that being more in tune to the lyrics and understanding the message of the songs I am singing help me to worship from a pure place. My thoughts of the words take me to a place in my heart that help me value and appreciate my personal relationship with Christ.

The second question I would ask myself is if in my haste to set the stage for my success, am I sure I am serving God? Most importantly, is it with my whole heart? Is desiring this success because I genuinely want to build a good customer base with what I have to offer that would help others?

Before we respond, let us consider this word from Matthew 7:21-23 (NIV).

> *"Not everyone who says to me, 'Lord, Lord,' will enter the kingdom of heaven, but only the one who does the will of my Father who is in heaven. Many will say to me on that day, 'Lord, Lord, did we not prophesy in your name and in your name drive out demons and in your name perform many miracles?' Then I will tell them plainly, 'I never knew you. Away from me, you evildoers!'"*

What's fascinating about this scripture is the things people do aren't bad. They just aren't flowing out of a relationship with Christ, which is bad. It was like they are using the things they do to gain favor or win God's approval.

Nothing is more important than you and me understanding that there is no amount of things you could ever do that will cause God to accept you or love you more. The way to the Father is through Jesus Christ—period. No other gimmicks, gadgets, magical way we can get there. It must be this way and on Christ's terms. Any other way is evil. Even though we don't often think of it in these terms, it is.

Another important question to ask ourselves is why is God's way so hard for us to accept? Could it be our pride, rebellion, our disobedience, or our failure to adhere to what matters most to God?

If we are serving, then we should be eager to let our service to Him flow out of our relationship with Him. We must serve Him because we love Him. You cannot try to serve Him to get God to love us.

Lastly, just like trying to be successful on our own with no help from God, we must consider this question. Are we the "Center of Your Own Show?" In other words, do we desire success so we can stand up and stick our chest out or place that degree on the wall and require everyone to call me Doctor This, as if we have arrived at the point of success on our own?

Once again, Matthew 6:1 (NIV) says, "Be careful not to practice your righteousness in front of others to be seen by them. If you do, you will have no reward from your Father in heaven." Now, if the possibility of going to heaven and living out eternity with God does not matter to you, then you have my permission to simply skip over this chapter altogether.

Jesus really jumps straight to the heart of the matter. Why are you doing what you are doing? You might say you're doing it for the right reason. But if you are doing it to be seen, then you already received your reward here on the earth. You have planted that seed of selfishness of thought in your heart. Jesus is encouraging us to be careful of the why, because when you know that it reveals what's really in your heart, it isn't too late to change that structure.

A close examination of (as a man thinks in his heart, so is he) can give us so much understanding. You and I need to always guard our hearts, paying close attention to what's in them. Our overall desire is to want to get to the place where everything we say is agreeing with everything that is truly in our heart.

Because, as we think, so are we.

Chapter Eighteen

The Lifter of my Head

I DISTINCTLY REMEMBER YEARS ago. I was struggling with a particular situation in my life. I was not sure how it was going to turn out for me in the end. I was in church, but I was allowing (unbeknownst to myself) the cares of the world in terms of how others saw or understood me overwhelm me.

I allowed their judgmental comments, off-centered jokes, and negative responses to shape my day and sometimes my life. Those years were painstaking and taxing to say the least. It seemed like the more I chased after God, the more the hellions sought after me for doing so.

Unfortunately, I spent entirely too many years worrying and carrying about the wrong things, and quite frankly, the wrong people in general. One of the first mistakes I made during this ordeal was to give too much strength to their take on my personal life and my walk with Christ from the outside.

Once, I was riding alone in my car, listening to the radio. This particular song came on, and the radio announcer introduced the song as "Jesus, Center of My Joy!"[1] Without hearing the first words, I literally broke down and cried. I mean the uncontrollable "I don't have nothing to lose" cry.

---

1. (Gloria Gaither, 1999)

By the time the artist, Richard Smallwood, began to sing, I knew in my heart of hearts, that is exactly where I wanted God to reign. Prior to this song's lyrics, I did not know how to phrase it. But the song said everything I wanted and needed it to say for me.

The way he sang it said everything. You could hear the sincerity in his voice and in the texture of his tone. I wanted Jesus as the center of my joy. I related to his comparison of Jesus as a compass when I've lost my direction. I could relate to those exact words, because that's what I was trying to figure out. Where did I go from that point in my life?

While I was trying my best to move forward, I was allowing life and the things around me to interject themselves into my life and my spiritual growth. They caused me at times to doubt myself and the things I was meant to accomplish.

Toward the end of the song, Richard pointed to Jesus as the source and finisher of dreams. The center of... me. There it was again. This calmness and resolve about the song message that simply ministered to my heart and soul.

I personally needed Jesus to become the center of my heart and life. Thinking of Jesus as being the lifter of my head is not just about me looking upward into the blue sky and hoping all things slowly but surely come together. I was learning to take small steps at a time, trusting God every day for ordering my steps.

The more I became involved in the studying of God's Word for my life, the more I saw the strategic plan I believed God had for me. This plan was not like everyone else's plan, and it was not designed to be.

Sometimes in life's journey, the road or the plan for one's life may become narrowed for a season at certain intervals. That does not mean it will be that way for the duration of your life. It just meant it was imperative that I follow close in keeping and hearing what God had to say for me to do.

There is truly a blessing in the obedience of hearing the voice of God. Even more important than hearing His voice is obeying what you have heard. Sometimes, it can be quite challenging to obey simply because of what you are seeing happen all around you. However, it is in those times you must keep forging ahead despite what you are feeling.

Admittedly, in the tough and uncertain times in which the world operates today, negative news, negative people, and in some cases, negative reactions and responses to the news surround us. There must be intentional focus to stay unmovable in the fight to stay true to the obedience of God.

I do not know about you, but I occasionally will have unsolicited advice given to me from others who have no genuine investment in me or my life. They tend to try to persuade me to override a decision I have made and go with the majority instead. Comments like, "Oh girl, go ahead and do it. Everyone else is doing it."

Even though my response back to them may appear to sound like a Debbie downer, I will not allow other's advice or suggestions to order my steps. At the end of the day, I am the one who will live with the outcome no matter what.

Now, I understand that one can live and have fun and enjoy their life and still remain a Christian. It is important to remember that "Christ died for all, that those who live should no longer live for themselves but for him who died for them and was raised again." 2 Corinthians 5:15 (NIV).

Faith is the bond of a living union with Jesus Christ by which Christ lives in you and me through the Holy Spirit. And the Christ who lives in you and me, came into the world to serve.

Think of the picture of sin as a man who is focused on himself. He is preoccupied with his own needs and problems, how other people have let him down, how he is going to make his mark in the world, and when he will get the break he deserves. Sin, at times, has us so focused on ourselves we cannot recognize anything else happening around us. Jesus came to save his people from their sins (see Matthew 1:21).

It is important to realize when Jesus, who was not focused on Himself, comes into a human life, He has an effect. He straightens us up. He saves us from loving, trusting, and serving ourselves. Christ lifts us up from preoccupation with ourselves, so when looking into the face of God, we are able to say, "I love you, I trust you, and I will serve you!"

In Psalm 3:3 (ESV), David says, "You are the lifter up of my head." In other words, "God, you deliver me from being consumed with myself and with my troubles. You deliver me from being my own god. You lift up my head so that, by faith, I can see You. You put your Spirit in me so I desire to serve others."

Faith unites us to the Christ who serves, so true faith will show itself in serving others with a cheerful heart. When I think of Jesus being the Lifter of my head, I think of support, guidance, deliverance, and being anchored in something far greater than myself.

From that scripture, I have come to understand that Jesus is not just up in heaven watching me below, merely observing but unwilling to help me along the way. When I think of Jesus being the lifter of my head, I think of him as desiring to share the load of life every step of the way. No matter what my day or night looks like, He is accommodating to me in every way.

Jesus' willingness to walk with me and be by my side is more than I can ever ask for. Just knowing the King of kings and the Lord of lords is my personal escort is a real game changer for me. He is my before, during, and after.

His will for my life is nothing short of a miracle within itself. He is my everything and then some. I live to serve. I will worship Him, and I live to do His uncompromising will. It is my total honor to just be in His presence.

Jesus being the Lifter of my head means I should not have any worries. Now, that doesn't mean I will not have to endure some things, but it does mean it is going to be alright. In fact, better than alright. It is going to be greater.

The Lifter of my head is the Owner of the cattle on a thousand hills. He's the Way Maker, The Heavy Load Bearer. He's the Healer,

The Comforter, The Way in, and the Way Out. He is the Lord of lords and the King of kings. He is the Everlasting God!

There is absolutely no one beside Him, no one before Him. No one that can outdo Him. No one that can control Him. He is the Alpha and the Omega. He is the Beginning and the Ending of it all. He is the only One that can sit up and put down. He is the door opener and the door closer.

There is no one that can come remotely close to Him, and the best part of it all, He is mine oh mine, and I am glad about it. I brag on Him. I boast on Him. I lean and depend upon Him.

One of the things I love about being a daughter of the Most High is He is never ashamed to show Himself strong in my life. He is not afraid to show Himself being all-powerful in my life. He is not afraid to allow harsh things to come against me, only to rise up and be the all-encompassing God and show the world He is still in control.

It is no secret what the Lord can do. What He does for one, He is more than capable of doing for others! Thank you, Jesus! I love that the thought of God being a Lifter of my head reminds me of the scripture from Psalms 3:3 (ESV). "But you, O Lord, are a shield about me, my glory, And the lifter on my head."

This scripture matters most to me. Like David wrote this beautiful Psalm during one of the darkest seasons of his life. Which is somewhat where I am treading right now in my life. This Psalm made me want to jump up and praise the Lord with everything within me.

This scripture reminded me I can allow it to become one of my personal prayers to God. I can pray it, asking Him to deliver me from my many excuses, doubts, second-guessing, drawbacks, and anything or anyone that wants to hold me down.

Jesus being the Lifter of my head reminds me to look back only temporarily and think about all the things that caused me to tremble, shake in my boots, question the power of God in and over my life. It helps me consider the times I allowed the whisper of the enemy to think this is the very best I could do and that my heart desires were only a wish.

Like David when he considered and reminisced about the history he had with God, his ascent to the throne of Isreal was difficult. Yet he could not help but remember all of his life had been filled with difficulty—especially prior to his time with God. However, the Lord fulfilled His promise to David.

As we look at this same scripture, many years later we find David's adult son, Absalom, desires his father's crown and exhibits rebellion and to assassinate his father. Heartbroken, dismayed, sad, and probably overwhelmed, David is forced to flee Jerusalem, the City of David.

David gives all the glory to God because he recognizes immediately that all his confidence comes from God. This, in turn, caused me to ask God to become the center of my world and my universe. I desire to have total confidence in God and His ability to Lord over my entire life and to work literally every situation out for my good.

Someone may ask me today, "Brenda, where is your confidence in the world today to move forward in the things God has called you to do?" My reply would be that daily I test my request when I pray to the Lord for His help and strength. I want Him to know my total dependence relies upon His name alone.

Without a shadow of a doubt, I find it humorous when I hear unbelievers say, "Religion is just a crutch for weak people."

Well, I would not call my relationship with the Lord a crutch. I will admit my weakness. I will gladly confess how frail and feeble I am. But rather than saying the Lord is a "crutch," I prefer David's description in Psalm 18:2 (ESV). "The LORD is my rock and my fortress and my deliverer, my God, my rock, in whom I take refuge, my shield, and the horn of my salvation, my stronghold."

Understanding that the Lord is a lifter of my head means I recognize that God is a total shield around me. Knowing and being aware of that lets me know I have nothing to fear except fear itself.

Another important verse I constantly meditate on is when David says in verse 1, "O Lord, how many are my foes! Many are rising against me." Absalom had created an entire army against his father.

Overwhelmed, David cries out to the Lord as he calculates how many are against him.

Have there been times you have felt this way? Do you know the sharp pain of betrayal? Rather than focusing on his enemies, David instead focuses on the Lord! After saying, "But You, O Lord," he then reminds the Lord that He is a "Shield" about him.

What an interesting way to pray. David was a man of war. He was well acquainted with the battlefield. He describes the Lord's protection as a shield. Thank you, Jesus.

Shields were very large in ancient warfare. They were made of solid wood, typically weighing approximately 40 pounds. They were the size of doors and strapped in leather. Some shields where so large that when arrows flew, two to three men could hide underneath them. What an incredible metaphor for God's protection over my life.

In that particular scripture alone, it makes me want to do a leap of joy, because I realize we face a far stronger enemy than Absalom. Our enemy is far greater and far more dangerous in the times in which we live.

Paul paints a vivid portrait in Ephesians 6:11-13 (ESV). "Put on the whole armor of God, that you may be able to stand against the schemes of the devil. For we do not wrestle against flesh and blood, but against the rulers, against the authorities, against the cosmic powers over this present darkness, against the spiritual forces of evil in the heavenly places. Therefore, take up the whole armor of God, that you may be able to withstand in the evil day, and having done all, to stand firm."

I love the part that says, "Take up the whole armor of God!" That means I must be willing not only to take notice, but I must make the deliberate choice to do so with intent to understand if God is for me, He is more than the whole world against me. Not only will I personally take up my shield, but I am more than willing to wear it proudly.

Yes, our enemy is fierce. He is strong. But the Lord promises us He is our shield of defense! We may be surrounded by a godless culture (this present darkness), we may be bombarded by temptations, tested by trials, and pressed by an enemy whose sole objective is to steal, kill, and destroy. But the Lord is a shield about us! He protects us from every side. Above, around, and beneath. He is our shield!

Hallelujah to my Wonderful King! He reigns, and nothing or no one can outdo Him, He is great and is worthy to be praised! I wondered about the reason David called the Lord his glory. Can't you see it was the Lord who took David from a lowly shepherd boy to the mighty King of Israel? It was God's doing alone.

Let me remind my readers of this part of the scripture. Do you remember David's story? The prophet Samuel came to David's house in 1 Samuel 16. When the prophet arrived, David's father, Jesse, lined up all his sons. David was missing, because he was tending the sheep in the fields. When Samuel examined each son, he had to ask Jesse if he had any other sons. Jesse, his own father, forgot about David.

Watch this. David was lowly. He was humble. He was a shepherd boy. But this shepherd boy knew the Great Shepherd. He was able to pen, "The Lord is my shepherd. I shall not want." (Psalm 23 KJV). When David appeared before Samuel, the Lord confirmed and showed Samuel David was to be anointed as the next King of Israel.

Now here is a very important moment to pay attention to. When David calls the Lord, "My glory," David is acknowledging that all he has comes from the Lord. God is the source of any honor or glory David possesses. Can you and I say the same? Absolutely.

I personally experience time and time again those days and years when I have done my very best. Worked some very long hours serving and giving in my servanthood, both to the people and unto God. My genuine service, whether in secular settings or in church, has more than often been taken advantage of—sometimes used and abused.

It didn't matter whether I understood what they were doing or not, it didn't seem to bother any of them. There were times when I have been overlooked, underpaid, looked over, picked over, and picked apart all because of my love and desire to serve the King of kings with my whole heart. I have been laughed at, called out, and talked about—sometimes all in the same day, but I still choose to serve Him. Just as David's glory was God chose him to be King, our glory is that God has chosen us to so great a salvation! Listen to Hebrews 7:25 (ESV). "Consequently, he is able to save to the uttermost those who draw near to God through him, since he always lives to make intercession for them."

Paul wrote in Ephesians 1:4-5 (ESV), "Even as he chose us in him before the foundation of the world, that we should be holy and blameless before him. In love he predestined us for adoption as sons through Jesus Christ, according to the purpose of his will."

We must learn to see how God is our glory, because He has lifted us from the pits of sin into his Kingdom. 1 Peter 2:9 (NIV) is very fitting. "But you are a chosen people, a royal priesthood, a holy nation, God's special possession, that you may declare the praises of him who called you out of darkness into his wonderful light."

It is imperative to fully understand that God alone is the Lifter of My Head. Period. Not only should David call the Lord, "The lifter of my head," but so should we. This is one of my favorite phrases in the entire Bible. It is a phrase I often use in my prayers. In personal worshipping and in my thanksgiving.

God will never be second in my life. No matter how challenging and no matter how overlooked and looked over. The world tries to make me believe they are running my life and either I bow and yield to them, or I will never achieve nor see the goodness of God for my life.

Think of the sorrow David felt as his own son tried to assassinate him. Think of the shame he felt leaving his city to flee this new army. What is the natural posture of depression and sorrow? It is to lower our head. David penned in Psalm 38:6 (KJV), "I am bowed down greatly, I go mourning all the day." Do you know seasons like this? Are you in a time of life when your head is down?

I want to remind you God is the "God of all comfort" (2 Corinthians 1:3) and the "Joy of the Lord is your strength" (Nehemiah 8:10). God has the ability to lift your head! He will come to your rescue. He will not fail. He is a shield about you. He knows how to deliver His people.

As a people of God, we must learn and train our mind to believe God over everything and everyone else no matter what. Let's challenge ourselves to pray in the same pattern as David did when he prayed, "But You, O Lord are a shield about me." This acknowledges God and that your faith and life are centered upon Him. God is our protector.

Psalm 5:11 (ESV) says, "But let all who take refuge in you rejoice; let them ever sing for joy, and spread your protection over them, that those who love your name may exult in you." Pray to the Lord, "My Glory." It is God's Name, His reputation on the line. He will come through, and He will give you His glory.

Lastly, let's pray, "The lifter of my head." Don't expect to stay in your depression. The Lord will lift your head. He will deliver you swiftly. Look to Him, call on Him, and trust in Him with all your heart.

Chapter Nineteen

From Restricted to Being Reserved

> *"Go into that village over there," he told them. "As you enter it, you will see a young donkey tied there that no one has ever ridden. Untie it and bring it here. If anyone asks, 'Why are you untying that colt?' just say, 'The Lord needs it.'" So, they went and found the colt, just as Jesus had said. And sure enough, as they were untying it, the owners asked them, "Why are you untying that colt?" And the disciples simply replied, "The Lord needs it." So, they brought the colt to Jesus and threw their garments over it for him to ride on.*
>
> Luke 19:30-35 (NLT)

SOMETIMES IN LIFE WHEN we are overlooked and passed over time after time, it can become quite difficult to wrap your brain around the why of it all. And if we are not careful, it may look as though you will never get ahead in life. You may come to expect the least of it all.

You accept that just receiving the crumbs is what you deserve, and this is probably the best God has for you. And little by little, we start to believe the lie and accept what the enemy within us and those around us may be saying about us—that this is as good as it gets.

When life becomes so challenging and difficult to make sense of, in the moment, we don't realize how easy of a prey and vulnerable we become to the predators that circle around us. We don't see how our hope and dreams are beginning to disappear right before our eyes, because our lives are being invaded and bombarded with all types of negative emotions and lies all designed to keep us grounded and out of the purposeful realm God has designed for us.

If we are going to receive the blessings God has aligned for our lives, we must find those individuals capable of encouraging us, motivating us, and stoking the fires God placed in us. We must come to terms with those things and those individuals who are literally there to drain all life from us and leave us washed up at the end of the day.

It is vital that during those turbulent times in our lives, it is not enough to simply survive our daily challenges. We must get to that place where striving becomes our second nature. We must learn how to stretch our faith in God to a point where we choose to soar rather than merely flutter on the ground now and then.

Often, when we find ourselves stuck behind the eight ball, rather than going to the Author and the Finisher of our souls, we look inward. We allow the enemy to plant seeds of doubt that we are incapable, inept, or too weak to carry out the will of God in our lives.

We are busy trying to make sense out of what does not make sense. We don't understand why it seems as though the harder we try to get ahead in life, the worse things seem to get. It doesn't matter how gifted or talented we are, we are never selected for anything of importance.

Over time, this can and will become a mental indictment to your mental state of mind. Before long, you may even come to accept that you don't deserve more or better. So it becomes easy to accept whatever is being handed down to you.

When we feel restricted in life, it is important to note that the people we choose to surround ourselves with directly shape our personal development. I have learned this by paying attention to those I have associated myself with.

Have you noticed that people in your life who don't mind hanging out with you when there is no one of importance to them around? However, as soon as you are no longer needed to serve their immediate purpose, you are not even an afterthought to them.

Have you ever wondered why you never hear from some people until they need something from you? Or when they are having a crisis of some sort, they already know no one else is going to give them a shoulder, arm, or leg to cry on. You, however, will stop your life and put yourself on hold to loan them your undivided attention for days with no problem.

Have you ever wondered how you are always the one at work to be given projects after projects but never get the credit or recognition you deserve? The only thing you do receive is the underserved criticism and negative write-ups about how your work was never up to par. Why are you the first person to be called on to do the hardest job and work the longest hours, to do the most? But you never get the proverbial time to talk about your work, because you are not good enough in their eyes.

I have watched those individuals who are more than eager and willing to step on, run down, steal, kill, lie, cheat, and sell their mothers out for the upper hand. Nothing is off the table. Nothing is too dirty. And nothing is too beneath them to sell you out to get what they want.

They will lie to you to your face. They will say and do just about anything to get what they want when they want it. Make no mistake, these are the people being promoted when they are not remotely qualified. That doesn't matter, because it is becoming the new norm. It doesn't matter that the morals are missing. The truth is overlooked, and integrity is obsolete, a thing of the past.

We must become sharply aware that the company you keep influences your thoughts, your behaviors, and ultimately, your future. You cannot afford to let negativity or mediocrity seep into your life, because your success, happiness, and self-worth depend on the energy that surrounds you.

I will be the first to admit that being overlooked and underappreciated is not an easy pill to swallow. Being used and mishandled is never a good feeling to undertake. This is why it is important to know your worth in Christ and not to allow yourself to surrender your integrity and anointing from God for 15 minutes of self-made fame for anything or anyone.

When we see people getting worldly recognition without the work ethics in place or the proverbial crown they made on their own, that is not the time to do a false celebration. For them it will be short-lived. This is the time when we must trust and rest in the Lord and in the power of His might, relying upon His supernatural power to withhold us and order our steps. I am fully aware of how the world makes fun of the church today. They laugh at anyone who still believes there is a God who sits on the throne. One of the reasons I think they may feel this way is because they do not readily see any of the ramifications of their actions.

I recently read an article on LinkedIn from *Daily Good News* that said the key to greatness lies in being intentional about the relationships you cultivate. Be relentless in choosing people who push you forward, who empower you, and who challenge you to be the best version of yourself. While I believe this is a true statement, I choose to believe we must ask God to place in our lives those individuals we are to walk and yoke up with that will help us shoulder the God-given loads assigned to us.

Our success is never a solo journey. It is built on the shoulders of encouragement, wisdom, and positive reinforcement. It is imperative that we surround ourselves with individuals who radiate confidence, integrity, and ambition. You absorb those same qualities.

But this type of support should run concurrently from one individual to another. It should never be one-sided or short-sighted. When we are in the right tribe or with people who support us, this is the type of drive that can inspire both parties to strive higher. Their honesty strengthens each other's character, and their belief in fuels each other's confidence. Both people can then rise to the level of improvement and success across the board.

So, it is imperative that each individual chooses wisely. If we desire to be great, we must walk with those who embody greatness. The question may be asked, "How do you stay positive when all around us in the world today is negative, negative, and even more negativity?"

We all should know by now that negative influences do more than just hold you back, they sabotage your potential. Toxic relationships, whether through doubt, deception, or discouragement, slowly erode your self-esteem and ambition. They affect your mindset, your emotions, and even your physical health in multiple ways.Even still, when negative things continuously happen to us, we can feel as though our lives are restricted at best. And when we feel restricted over time, we have the tendency to give up and become bewildered. Sometimes, we even give up or give in to the cares of this world.

When we think of the words "restricted or restriction," we find, according to Cambridge.org, restriction is "the **act of putting a limit or control on something**." It can refer to a regulation that restricts or restrains, or a limitation on the use or enjoyment of property or a facility. Restriction can also refer to the state of being restricted. Examples of restrictions include the concentration of retailing, which could lead to restriction of choice, higher prices, and reduced accessibility. [1]

The biblical definition of Restricted is found in the Topical Encyclopedia to reflect the biblical concept of restriction often being related to the limitations or boundaries set by God for humanity's benefit, protection, and spiritual growth. These restrictions can be seen in various forms, including commandments, laws, and divine

---

1. (Cambridge University Press, n.d.)

instructions, which are intended to guide believers in living a life that is pleasing to God.[2]

When we look at the word reserve, it means "to keep something for a particular purpose or time. To arrange for something to be kept for your use at a later time. The act of keeping something or a supply of something until it is needed. To keep back or set aside, especially for future use or contingency. To keep for oneself; retain or to obtain or secure by advance arrangement."[3]

"In biblical terminology, the concept of "reserved" often pertains to God's sovereign will and His divine plan, where certain things are set apart for specific purposes or times. This notion is woven throughout Scripture, illustrating God's control over creation and His unfolding plan for humanity."[4]

Luke 19:31-37 (NLT) reads, "Go into that village over there," he told them. "As you enter it, you will see a young donkey tied there that no one has ever ridden. Untie it and bring it here. If anyone asks, 'Why are you untying that colt?' just say, 'The Lord needs it.' So, they went and found the colt, just as Jesus had said. And sure enough, as they were untying it, the owners asked them, 'Why are you untying that colt?' And the disciples simply replied, 'The Lord needs it.' So, they brought the colt to Jesus and threw their garments over it for him to ride on."

What a very powerful scripture to read and allow to sink into your heart and your thoughts. This verse is very meaningful to me. "The Lord has need of him" signifies a phrase from the Bible used in the context that states, the "Master" has need of him. Period. Sometimes in life, you may wonder what your real purpose for existence is. This

---

2. (Topical Encyclopedia)

3. (Cambridge University Press, n.d.)

4. (Topical Encyclopedia, n.d.)

discovery could take years to really find out. You may try various things on your own, searching it out. You may even depend upon others close to you for help to figure it out, which can most often cause undue stress and anxiety, doubt, and fears.

My personal discovery in reading this verse is that the colt was indeed created for a specific and special purpose. But he, like all of us, had to wait for that appropriate moment in time the "Master" had carved out—that time for him to go from being hidden and undiscovered to being loosed and free to be seen and exposed for the Master's use.

It appears to me this colt merely went from the possibility of being displaced, overlooked, undervalued, unappreciated, unworthy, underrated, underestimated, and unimportant for anything worthwhile. All its existence had been spent tied up. Limited. Restricted and kept on a monitor as an "if all else fails" mechanism. We could possibly use him at that point. Until then, he remains restricted and regulated.

One of the other values I see in this scripture is the importance of keeping a positive composure when you are in uncertain times about your purpose. It is such a daily fight to remain positive and to keep your head up when you are unsure about everything. You find yourself not only questioning your self-worth, but you also have questions about where you belong or even if you belong.

Think about it daily as you are looking around and watching everyone else being selected for certain tasks and responsibilities. Your name is not mentioned once, thought of, or announced, as if you are invisible.

Not only that, but you not worthy of an explanation or told the reasoning of why you are constantly overlooked and not remotely considered. Why do others think you should be devalued for anything meaningful? Why are not the same windows of opportunities offered to you as they are graciously and openly given to others.

The pang, hurt, torture, and daily disappointments you face from day-to-day can be almost unbearable to comprehend. Not only that, have you noticed whenever you are not included, others will quickly disassociate themselves with you? The truth of the matter is no one wants to be associated with someone they deem unimportant or consider a loser. They do not want to be seen with someone they feel is not moving forward or has anything of importance to add or contribute to the world.

I cannot help but believe in this colt's waiting period, it experienced difficulty, gut wrenching and painstakingly loneliness. He could not even buy a friend. For days, weeks, months, and possibly years, he spent his days and nights filled in misery, agony, and heartache.

He no doubt questioned the day he was born. He probably beat himself up and asked the notorious questions like we do, "Lord, why? Why me? What did I do to deserve this lot in life?" I don't know which is worse—asking the questions or not receiving any answers.

When you are drowning in silence, the wait can be crushing and unbearable and often too much for one person to carry. The wait can become overwhelming and all-consuming. You are at a complete loss for words and sometimes faith.

Everything becomes a fight to stay positive, a fight to remain faithful, and a fight to believe anything is remotely possible for you. You look around are completely and utterly alone in your limited and confined space with just your thoughts and opinions.

I would imagine the colt's eyes were tender from the shedding of many tears. Here he is being intentionally left alone to fend for himself, draw his own conclusions about the outcome of his life, and no one to encourage him or pour life into him. He probably thought he was at least owed an explanation of he was forced to live in obscurity and utter despair. Shunned by his peers and overlooked by family members who no longer wanted to associate themselves with him, they never came around. At this point, the colt didn't know what to believe or expect. He, no doubt, was almost at his wits end.

But then Jesus, in His appointed time, pulled out all the stops. He sent people into the village to do a job. He gave them specific instructions, He told them, "As you enter it, you will see a young donkey tied there that no one has ever ridden. Untie it and bring it here."

Look at the power and authority in Jesus' voice. He didn't shout or rant and scream. Nor did He ask. He merely spoke and put a demand on it. Everyone had no choice but to comply. What a Mighty and Powerful God we serve.

Not only did Jesus command them to bring the unsuspecting, scared colt to Him, but He also answers the question of the gentleman to whom the colt belong before he even asked.

Jesus goes further by saying, "If anyone asks, 'Why are you untying that colt?' just say, 'The Lord needs it.'" Now that's the kind of God I truly serve. No one can override Him, no one can outdo Him, and no one can overrule Him. He alone is God all by Himself. He has the whole world in His hands.

Look at the preciseness of Jesus' request of the men. He did not send them on a wild-goose chase. Jesus sends them directly to where the little colt was tied up as he had been for years. When the men arrived at the appointed place, they found exactly what Jesus said.

The scripture continues and says, "So, they went and found the colt, just as Jesus had said." And sure enough, as they were untying it, the owner asked them, "Why are you untying that colt?" Not only was the colt in place but the men found him still tied up, restricted, limited, controlled, constrained, and confined.

Look at this, the colt had an owner, but the owner was also the one who tied him up. The owner restricted him. The colt had a place to stay, but it was the owner who made his space limited. The colt was told the owner had an agenda for his life. But upon closer examination, the colt found out he would only be lead about in small circles round and round again.

Then, I can see in my spiritual mindset, the Lord. He is the plan, knows the real plan, orchestrated the plan, put the plan together, had a need for His plan, and called His plan together and placed it in action.

Only God can "set" a plan in motion and place a spiritual timer on it. He alone places a spiritual demand on it and sets the clock for our lives and the spiritually appointed time. In the right atmosphere, at the precise moment, and when it pleases God, He calls it into action.

The Bible does not give a specific date or time. The Word simply said, "The Lord needs it." Now, it is important for us to understand the Lord's needs are totally different from ours. Our needs are oftentimes nothing but a glorified want.

Have you ever seen a child crying for more when he or she already has a fist full of chips in the left hand? Wailing and stomping his or her feet, the right hand lifts begging for more of something he or she really does not need. Something the child already has enough of. Crying before partaking of what's already been given freely. The child throws a temper tantrum, screaming for something that does not belong to him or her, but simply wants it out of greed.

If you were to confront the child and ask what's wrong, the reply mostly will be "No." The head shakes, tears rolling down, and screaming louder without an admission or acknowledgment of the truth that nothing is wrong. They just want their way.

That is the way life is in some cases. You may find yourself in a marriage that once was magical. But through the years, it became less like a real protected and safe space to land and became more like a war zone, where nothing as you knew it any longer felt right.

Have you ever felt you worked so hard at a company and gave your life's blood to the cause? You came in early and stayed late. You worked your job and others' too. Maybe you took on the brunt and the grunt work no one else wanted to do.

You applied for positions of upward mobility only never to be interviewed or given a reason why you were not a good fit for the position. Months pass and you hear through the grapevine throughout the office you were not qualified. You find yourself wondering why you always felt like a misfit, unrecognizable even though you always remained visible. You may have asked yourself repeatedly, "what's wrong with me? What have I done wrong?" Even the proverbial, "Why me?"

You may feel as though the more good you put out into the world it seems trails, tribulations, heartache, and pain is always lunging at your heels. Day after day, you come to fully understand that grace and mercy has been your only friend.

Like the colt that was tied up, I can only imagine the sheer agony, betrayal, and low self-esteem that must have built up over the years of his lonely life. No one around him to encourage him. No one willing to properly invest in him. And no one came out to pet or ride him, or even spend quality time with him. All he had to look forward to was being tied up.

I could imagine the colt thought his life was a mistake, not worthwhile, wasted, and perhaps a colossal joke—especially when he could not figure out why his entire world was always lived as a standalone. He could not connect the dots as to what made the other animals more special than him.

What could "he" do differently to turn the outcome of his life? He thought to himself if it was necessary, he could try to blend in or do everything he could do to fit in with all the other animals. The colt may have even considered he could dumb his life and light down so others would see he is just like them. If that's what it took to become loosed and free to live like others who appeared free to roam, he would.

The more the colt pleaded and imagined his life as better, the more he was left alone to dream about the possibilities of what he could only imagine. Freedom and acceptance.

I imagine no matter how strong you are, how prayed up you are, how much you love Jesus, life will come for you. At times, it will wrestle you and your strength to the ground. It will watch you ache and thrash about in relentless pain and sorrow with such despair and find yourself questioning every move.

In your lonely hours, you may feel time and chance have passed you by. You wonder if anything good can come from your limited and meager beginnings. You think to yourself, if only I had someone I could trust to share my heart and trials with, perhaps I could be revived enough to continue the journey, no matter where it leads me.

He was afraid to believe again and to hold out hope. His faith had been stretched beyond human measure, and at this point in the life of the colt, he had become accustomed to heartache and pain. He considered discomfort as a distant friend and had just began to accept his supposed lot in life.

Like the colt, just when his life was beginning to feel unbearable and unsettling, an unexpectant turn of events appeared seemingly out of nowhere. The colt could hardly believe his eyes. He had been down for so long. He was too afraid to allow himself to accept even the smallest possibility that his life was about to change for the better.

Then one day, suddenly his life was about to change drastically. The colt had no earthly idea what was happening to him. While he must have experienced various emotions at this time, he was curious about what, if anything, this new discovery had to do with him.

Not being able to get a read on the two gentlemen's faces as they quickly approached the village, he wanted desperately to understand what was about to happen to him. But he could not.

Finally, the suspense of it all was about to come to a head, and the colt was about to understand what the next step in his journey would be. After the gentlemen had reached the village, further instructions had already been given to them to follow.

Wow! What a game changer.

At the appointed time in a lowly village, for the first time in this colt's life, he hears good news. He can hardly believe it. His ears perk up, and curiosity gives him confidence that today could possibly be the day when everything turns around for him. With that glimmer of hope, the colt's legs gain strength. A new world opens for him. At this point, it is important to note that while it was exciting the colt was being discovered, it is even more beneficial to note by whom the colt was being discovered.

The colt was freed from his devastating turmoil that kept him bound and limited for years. Think about it. For years, the colt was made the laughingstock of all the surrounding farms animals. Daily his life was scrutinized and kept under a microscope to be examined by other animals at will. But that day, can you imagine the rumor was going wild? Gossip and accusations filled the air.

"Oh, my goodness, have you all heard the latest news about the colt next door? You know the one who wasn't very useful? The one that has been tied up for years and wasn't allowed to roam about?"

"Oh, him? The one I heard was not very healthy or smart. The one who was never doing anything. All he did was stand or sit there under this shade tree and walk around in small circles. Who in the world could have been interested in him? Does anyone know?"

You and I know gossip, lies, and deception travels faster than any good praise report any day, because the average person loves to hear the negative rather than encouragement.

Imagine that as the good news spread around the farmyard, the other animals could not believe what they were hearing. They came closer to listen in on the conversation as to the whereabouts of the little colt. I can almost hear the other animals laughing, cracking jokes in utter disbelief, possibly laying bets that this is going to be good. This is going to be the funniest thing they heard in a very long time.

Another animal chimes in a thought. "Yeah, when has any of us seen the little colt do anything incredible or meaningful before?"

When the other animals arrived at the appointed time and space where the little colt, not even a thought on the Richter scale, was no longer present, they were shocked. They realized the unassuming colt had left his one-dimensional lifestyle for a different pasture without the aid or assistance from any of them. They were utterly confused and bewildered.

None of the other animals could take credit for his assistance. None of the other animals could brag about "had it not been for me, the little undeveloped, no named colt would not be what could possibly be today."

No one could get the credit, the glory, the honor, the praise, the bragging rights, or the notoriety but God. It was God who sent His word into the village to summon the insignificant colt and bring him to the Lord.

Can you not see the great Arm of God resting upon this beat-down, discouraged animal? Little did they know, they were going to be in for a rude awakening. They colt was not simply untied to roam about the farmyard on its own. No, the colt was untied by the command of Jesus and asked to be brought to Him for the Master's use.

"Why?" you may ask. Because the Lord had need of him. I do not know about you, but there is absolutely nothing in this world sweeter than being kept separated and reserved for the Master's use, because there is no other Name like His.

This was life changing for the colt. He never could have envisioned anything of this nature for his life. In fact, he didn't see this coming. But he was excited this moment had finally arrived for him.

Chapter Twenty

Resting in Wait

WE ALL KNOW WAITING is never easy for the best of us. No one in the world likes to wait or even have the thought of waiting for anything. The thought of waiting nowadays sounds like the most absurd thing in the world.

We see it everywhere today, but especially in traffic, at the grocery stores, work, doctors office, and you name it. Most struggle with having patience and waiting.

Personally, I do not have the greatest patience when it comes to waiting. But I will confess that, by the grace of God, I have come a very long way in my effort to do better and become more tolerate of it.

I have to admit, I often ask myself why a struggle is there in the waiting. What is it about the waiting process that makes it a challenge for me? I am discovering it is in the silence of it all, not knowing exactly what is lurking around the corner. Will it be good or bad news? What will the outcome mean for me?

Thinking about it sometimes can cause me to become anxious and worried. Unable to come up with answers of my own while I am waiting makes me feel completely inadequate and sometimes helpless.

Over the years, when I have found myself in this realm of waiting, I am learning how to turn to God and lean on Him in my weakness and fear of the waiting process. I cry out to him for strength and fortitude in the wait. I ask Him to teach me and help me rest in Him while, in the meantime, I believe He is working out everything needed in both me and my situation.

Right now, everything seems shaken up. Nothing is exactly as we have been accustomed to. Everywhere we look, change is taking place at rapid speeds. How we work, where we work, how we worship, and where we worship. How we grocery shop and how our food can be delivered. It's just different.

Waiting without what I call the right tools and support can be devastating for some and totally overwhelming for others. Especially when they "believe" they are in the waiting room all alone, and no one knows they are hurting.

Waiting is more than not moving or being idle and not doing anything or making any progress. Waiting is more a process all by itself. I am discovering it takes a certain mindset to tunnel through this very isolated journey.

I believe waiting is not the absence of strength or faith. Strength is not always required. Waiting is more about the willingness to surrender to God and submit myself and the things that cause me worry unto God, allowing Him to work those things out in me first and then through me.

I once heard a sermon on trusting God's timing for your life. The explanation given resonated with me on several levels that caused me to revisit my patience during this entire process.

Recorded in my notes while listening to the sermon by Pastor Charles Stanley, he mentioned that while we are waiting in God, it is important to believe first and foremost that we can trust God's timing in it all. He went further by saying this is not a time when we are so concerned with when this will all be over or I will have my questions answered. Rather, I am placing both myself and the problem in the hands of God and trusting Him alone to work all things out for my good.

Pastor Stanley said to acknowledge God's timing in the wait may not align with our expectations, but His plans are always for our good.

The question may be raised, "But what if I lose out in the wait? Or what if I feel as though I may get the low end of the stick when everything is over?" I may feel as though the wait was a colossal waste of my time.

Ecclesiastes 3:11 (KJV) says, "He hath made everything beautiful in its time: also, he hath set the world in their heart, so that no man can find out the work that God maketh from the beginning to the end."

As I study this verse, I realize it emphasizes that everything has an appointed time and beauty, and it reflects on the human inability to comprehend God's work throughout time. In other words, I am learning it is not enough to simply read the word of God and walk away with my interpretation of what I "think" the Word of God is saying to me. It's the choice to trust God's Word for my life and situation, believing God really loves me and is walking me through the process of the waiting period. Understanding that what God wants from me in this moment is to believe He knows me and wants nothing more for my life than the very best.

The blessing really is in the patience of waiting, because waiting on God can be challenging. Especially if you are an individual who must know the outcome before you can move forward or let something go. I don't have to tell you this, but if you are this type of individual with God, you probably have guested it by now. You are not going to win.

With God, there is a blessing in the waiting, because it is essential to remain expectant and grounded in prayer. Trusting God during these times helps us grow in faith. And as we grow in faith, we can receive the benefit God has in place for us as we relinquish our way to God's best.

Looking back over some specific times in my life, when I was trying to figure things out on my own, I can see now how much time I wasted driving myself crazy. I tried to put two and two together instead of choosing to believe God in the midst of it all when none of it made sense.

Now that I am growing more in my faith, I am coming to the conclusion that as I continue to wait on God, I will gain greater insight in my understanding of God's Sovereignty. I will recognize that God's wisdom surpasses my understanding. Proverbs 3:5 (NKJV) encourages us to "Trust in the Lord with all your heart and lean not to your own understanding."

During the waiting period, it allows my faith to rest in the promises of God even in the midst of uncertainty. As I accept the uncertainty of timing as a part of God's greater plan for my life, I chose to believe that God is always working behind the scenes for my personal benefit. It makes it easier for me to wait.

As out of sorts as things are in my life right now, I am leaning into the Word of God more and more. Daily it is becoming my compass and my sure thing. I am learning how to trust and seek the face of the Lord above anything and anyone else.

I know for myself that Psalm 23 has become my closest companion during these uncertain times in the world. Daily, I am seeking the face of the Lord more for my life as I draw closer to Him. When I recite the words of that Psalm, it brings me joy and renews my faith. I love reading this passage.

> *"The Lord is my Shepherd; I shall not want. He leads me beside the still waters. He restoreth my soul; he leadeth me in the paths of righteousness for his name's sake. Yea, though I walk through the valley of the shadow of death, I will fear no evil; for thou art with me; thy rod and thy staff they comfort me. Thou preparest a table before me in the presence of mine enemies; thou anointest my head with oil; my cup runneth over. Surely goodness and mercy shall follow me all the days of my life: and I will dwell in the house of the Lord forever." (KJV)*

In life, I have personally experienced various hardships and unexpected setbacks that have been painful to bear and to walk through. I must admit that while I didn't understand why some of those hardships were permitted by God, I still chose to look unto Him. I knew beyond a shadow of a doubt I'd rather risk everything I am in Him than trying to go it alone.

During hard times, it's easy to wonder why the Lord is taking so long to bring relief while your heart is broken. While you are hurting so badly or even when you feel as though your world has been turned upside down and you have no one to help you bear your cross.

Still, like the psalmist in Psalm 130:1, we cry to God "out of the depths" for help. But as time drags on, we may be tempted to take matters into our own hands. Believers, however, are not to operate as the world does, determining a course of action based on human reasoning or the example of others. Instead, our guidance is to come from God, and our hope is to be in His Word (see Psalm 130:5-6).

It's important that we cooperate with Him so the time spent waiting will prove productive and beneficial. God can use such "holding patterns" to reveal sinful behaviors or thoughts and to develop new heart attitudes. Waiting can also provide an opportunity to deepen our trust and dependence on Him. And when we follow God's timetable, He gives us the grace to endure difficult situations with confidence and peace. It's a blessing to know we're where God wants us, and He's promised to take care of us.

Let me personally encourage you. While reading my book if you're in God's waiting room, remember He is your hope—and in His time He will move you forward. Wait on Him even when life does not make sense. Wait on Him even when it feels as though your world is caving in. Still, chose to wait.

He may not come through when you want Him to, but He will always come through on time.

Chapter Twenty-One

The Tour Guide Knows the Route

"You know where you have been, but you don't know where you are going."
                                                    Frances Little

I CAN REMEMBER AS far back as over seven years ago. My mother, Frances Little, spoke this quote at various times during the week. Often, when she would be walking through her house or under stress, she would take a deep breath, hands placed on her hips and eyes closed. "You know where you have been, but you do not know where you are going!"

Because Mom would say this so often, I became curious, so one day, I decided to ask her about it.

Her reply was, "Babe, you can always look back and see how far you have come and how far the Lord has brought you; but you have no idea what you may have to walk through to get to where you have to go."

I cannot tell you how many times I wish my mother was still alive so I could finish that conversation with her to tell her just how accurate her words really were. In fact, her words were more than true. At least in my ears, they were spot on and are well and alive today.

I do not know a person alive who has not made at least some level of plans for their immediate future. Daily, people can be heard saying, "Tomorrow, I will do this or that, or I will be on vacation in March, April, or May. I will be out of town on this date. I will be retiring within the next six months."

We give no real thought about God's timing for our lives. We simply schedule what we want to happen and assume He will comply with our agenda. But our ways are not God's according to Isaiah 55:8-9 (NKJV). "'For My thoughts *are* not your thoughts, nor *are* your ways My ways,' says the Lord. 'For *as* the heavens are higher than the earth, So are My ways higher than your ways, And My thoughts than your thoughts.'"

According to Topical Encyclopedia, "the concept of the mystery of God's ways is a profound theme woven throughout the Scriptures, reflecting the divine nature and the limitations of human understanding. The Bible frequently acknowledges that God's thoughts and methods are beyond human comprehension, inviting believers to trust in His wisdom and sovereignty."[1]

Only God can take a situation that is rendered horrific or hopeless and turn it around for our good. Only God can change the heart of the king. He is the only One that provides us with uncommon favor even when everything around us, including ourselves, has failed. God is able.

In the beginning, according Genesis 1:1-3 (NIV), "God created the heavens and the earth. Now the earth was formless and empty, darkness was over the surface of the deep, and the Spirit of God was hovering over the waters. And God said, 'Let there be light,' and there was light."

Let's stop and try to wrap our minds around this concept. There was absolutely nothing and no one alive to add or contribute

---

1. (Topical Encyclopedia, n.d.)

anything to the creation of the world. There were no outside interferences, and no other input was needed.

It was God alone who set His plan into motion. He alone knew exactly what He wanted to accomplished and orchestrated it all from the beginning to the end. Only God knows the true plans He has set in motion for our lives. No one or nothing can change, interrupt, or usurp the ways of it. There is no One above Him, no One outside of Him, and no One that can change His mind toward us.

He alone is the absolute Tour Guide. All that place their trust and their hope in Him will never have to worry about the route God will lead them, no matter what. We can be assured that our God always finishes what He alone has started. He never shows us the entire thing from the beginning to the end, because He wants His believers to take Him at His word and to surrender ourselves over to Him.

In life and throughout His Word, God tells us He alone knows the specific plans He has for us. Even though those plans may include heartache, disappointments, hurt, embarrassment, loss of various kinds, and rerouting what we had envisioned for our lives, God is never lost in the details. He will cause everything to work out for us in the end.

It is challenging to wrap our heads around what our personal routes in life will entail, because we do not have a natural road map to follow. There is nothing that says or seems to indicate each day that you are here on your personal route. The only place we have to go is the Word of God if we are to fully embrace how we are going to walk through this world. Jeremiah 29:11 (NIV) tells us, "'For I know the plans I have for you,' declares the Lord, 'plans to prosper you and not to harm you, plans to give you hope and a future.'"

Now, you may be tempted to say, "Well that sounds good in theory. But how am I to rely upon that in the natural and in my everyday life? How am I supposed to depend upon that when I am not 100% sure this is true for my life?"

Well, that's just the point. We are not the leader of our path or our own way. We don't have the whole world in our hands. We don't know what tomorrow holds, and we certainly cannot do anything about it—even if we had the inside scoop.

Our total dependency is on God whether we want to believe it or not. God takes care of each of us every day. If it were not for His grace and mercy, we would not be able to function nor have the presence of our being.

It is easy for people to merely overlook God's goodness, because most people have no earthly clue or have ever discovered God's goodness for themselves. They have no idea it is God who causes the sun to rise in the morning and the moon to shine at night. They do not know it is Him who makes all things possible, and without His power in their life, they would be utterly destroyed and non-existent. They do not fully understand He is the One who rains on the just like He does the unjust.

Jesus is the One who forgives all of our sins and heals all of our diseases, and He cares so deeply for each of us. Jesus is not just someone who looks over us from afar, but He longs to be a part of our every move. He desires to live within us if we only allow Him to.

People do not recognize that God is the One who helps us every step of the typical day from our uprising until our lying down. Sometimes, our focus is so off we only call upon the name of God when we have come to the end of ourselves. When we've used up all our bag of tricks in our heavy-laden bags and briefcases we carry around daily.

We have a tendency to think, to believe, that we have somehow carved out our way in life and made it this far by personal efforts and smarts. We have bought into thinking that if God was real, only good things would be happening to us, and He would be more than willing to grant our every wish and make all our dreams come to. No questions asked.

When those outlandish and farfetched requests are not granted, we become upset, rude, angry, and disappointed. We eventually walk away from anything else the Word of God could possibly offer.

We spend tireless days, weeks, months, and sad years trying desperately to make our way in life. We don't believe or desire to accept help from anyone, because we think we don't need anyone else to help us.

It appears exciting for us to tell others about our successes and how we made it all happen. We recall the story over and over again to anyone willing to listen—how we personally pulled ourselves up by our bootstraps. We are filled with the personal pronoun of "I" syndrome of the I's have it.

There is something about pride that will not allow us to be humble or dependent on anyone but ourselves. For some, it is most difficult to acknowledge they may need assistance along the way. They may feel that asking others for help or direction along the way is a sign of weakness or insecurity.

Some, because of their hurts and disappointments, carry such a fear of ever trusting anyone else. They would rather walk alone and risk making mistakes than to turn to others for advice or direction. So they go through life suffering and carrying the load alone.

Here's the thing. Jesus simply wants to share the load with us. He already knows our beginning from our ending. After all, He is the One who created the plan for our lives, anyway. So, honestly, there is nothing hidden from Him. He is fully mindful of who we are, where we are headed, and exactly when or if we will arrive.

His desire for us, if we are willing to invite Him in and ask and accept His help, is to prosper us. "See how very much our Father loves us, for he calls us his children, and that is what we are! But the people who belong to this world don't recognize that we are God's children because they don't know him. Dear friends, we are already God's children, but he has not yet shown us what we will be like when Christ appears. But we do know that we will be like him, for we will see him as he really is." (1 John 3:1-2 NLT)

Following Jesus is not just following any ole round the way leader. To begin with, let's look at Jesus' demonstrative leadership qualities through following His traits.

His truthfulness. We can trust Jesus because He always spoke the truth. His compassion, because He was motivated by His compassion to lead us forward. His humility and His willingness to humble himself and follow God's will even to death on the cross for our sake. We don't just have a leader in Jesus but a risk-taking Jesus who humbled himself in His desire to follow God's will to the cross at Calvary for us.

Another notable reason, Jesus is a tour guide who can be trusted as our leader. We can look at Jesus' life as a Servant Leader, and His Leadership in and of itself is impeccable. Jesus defined greatness as being a servant and shared responsibility and authority with others. An important aspect of being a great leader is demonstrating humility, which Jesus did. He humbled himself and followed God's will. He took risks to serve others. He always forgave others without fail. And through His eagerness to forgive, He sat a foundation for leadership through love and grace.

One of the main attractions to great leadership is taking time to look at what traits make a good leader. Especially when it comes to life and particularly in our day-to-day life, we often find ourselves being confronted with choices about whom or what we should follow or admire.

As human beings, we're drawn to leaders with specific opinions and ideologies, and these choices can significantly shape our lives for the future. But in all our choices and thoughts about the future, we have an opportunity to look at Jesus for guidance.

What does Jesus have to teach us about what an honorable leader looks like?

Jesus shows us wise, loving leadership—this may be so different from many earthly leaders it can seem foolish to even try to compare them. But before we consider our current leaders, we should start by comparing Jesus to our thoughts, actions, and character traits.

In the natural or the world, we must acknowledge that no one gets it right every time. We have unending opportunities to practice giving and receiving forgiveness. We ask God to help us speak the truth in love and value people who are labeled worthless, those who treat us poorly, and even people who disagree with us. Instead of being led by our desire to be right, we can let compassion motivate our actions. We can forgive—even before being asked. We can be like the leaders we want to see.

Here are six characteristics of why I personally chose Jesus to become my personal tour guide. I hope this will be a blessing to you, too.

Jesus always speaks the truth without fear of repercussions. Jesus asks for more and offers more. While Jesus says His yoke is easy and His burden light (Matthew 11:30), His plan has a steep joining fee. He says, "Whoever wants to be my disciple must deny themselves and take up their cross and follow me." (Matthew 16:24 NIV).

May our commitment to Jesus be far greater than our commitment to earthly leaders, even when following Him is difficult. Jesus values us more. Why is Jesus willing to tell us to deny ourselves and follow Him? Because He loves us, and that's what it will take to have a relationship with Him.

Unlike a political candidate, Jesus doesn't need our support. He wants our company. He wants to enjoy life with us starting here on Earth and continuing into eternity—an offer no earthly leader can match.

Jesus values us so much He paid our debt of sin with His death. The author of Hebrews tells us, "For the joy set before him he endured the cross, scorning its shame." (Hebrews 12:2 NIV). The joy of fellowship with us was greater to Him than the pain of the cross. And He doesn't stop there! He's still seeking us, still calling us. He can't be stopped, because His love for us is relentless.

Jesus values all of us. No other leader can boast that. We've likely experienced the type of leader that seeks to surround themselves with influential people, hoping some of that influence will rub off on them. If we're looking to have an influence on Earth, hanging out with the smart, the beautiful, and the rich is a good strategy. That is what earthly leaders boast.

But it's not how Jesus operates. He not only spends time with people the world rejects, but He also goes looking for them. He seeks out the ostracized, poor, sick, weak, and people deemed "worthless."

Jesus is motivated by compassion. Our leaders can create amazing change when they allow compassion to motivate them to action. Most of us can understand what it's like to be compelled to act by compassion. We see people hurting, and we want to help. But Jesus is the compassion champion. He lets compassion mess up His plans, frustrate His followers, and throw His work-life balance out of whack.

We see this clearly right after John the Baptist's death. Jesus withdraws to a remote area to be alone (Matthew 14:13). So often surrounded by crowds, Jesus wanted to be alone after the death of someone important to Him. But the crowds of people heard where He was going, and rather than giving Him space, they followed and pressed in around Him, eager to have their needs filled.

When we're already tired or sad, the last thing we want is to be confronted by other people's demands, and we often react harshly. But Jesus looked out at the crowds and "had compassion on them and healed their sick" (Matthew 14:14 NIV). He set personal needs aside to minister to others, not because He had to, but because His compassion made Him want to.

Another wonderful attribute to a great leader is being assured that Jesus forgives. We can pray Jesus will inspire leaders to be moved by compassion. All over the world, we need to hold our leaders accountable, but true repentance should be met with true forgiveness. That kind of forgiveness sets us free to be the people God created us to be.

Jesus doesn't forgive to "be nice" or because it's the socially acceptable thing to do, He forgives to set people free. He doesn't want anything blocking people from living life in all its fullness (John 10:10).

In the end, we seek for true leaders who are relevant tour guides but who fully understand and are experts in knowing the exact route to lead us home. May we value leaders who are willing to forgive, and may we forgive them and not hold grudges that grow bitterness.

Your Thoughts and Reflections

Use this space to record thoughts, feelings, and scriptures related to this book.

References

Are Baby Ears More Sensitive? A Parent's Guide to Sound. (2025, Nov 18). Retrieved from Good Parents Blog: https://goodparents.blog/baby-ears-sensitive-sound-guide

Cambridge University Press. (n.d.). *Reserve in Cambridge Dictionary.* Retrieved Jan 6, 2026, from Cambridge Dictionary: https://dictionary.cambridge.org/dictionary/english/reserve

Cambridge University Press. (n.d.). *Restriction in Cambridge Dictionary.* Retrieved Jan 6, 2026, from Cambridge Dictionary: https://dictionary.cambridge.org/dictionary/english/restriction

Gloria Gaither, R. S. (1999). Center of My Joy [Recorded by R. Smallwood]. USA.

Grudem, W. (1994). *Systematic Theology: An Introduction to Bible Doctrine.* Leicester, England: Inter-Varsity Press.

Topical Encyclopedia. (n.d.). *Mystery of God's Ways in Topical Encyclopedia.* Retrieved Jan 6, 2026, from Bible Hub: https://biblehub.com/topical/t/the_mystery_of_god's_ways.htm

Topical Encyclopedia. (n.d.). *Reserved in Topical Encylopedia.* Retrieved Jan 6, 2026, from BibleHub: https://biblehub.com/topical/r/reserved.htm

Topical Encyclopedia. (n.d.). *Restricted.* Retrieved Jan 6, 2026, from BibleHub: https://biblehub.com/topical/r/restricted.htm

Wellum, K. (n.d.). *Trusting God.* Retrieved from The Gospel Coalition (TGC) U.S. Edition: https://www.thegospelcoalition.org/essay/trusting-god/

About the Author

BRENDA MURPHY is a captivating and inspirational Christian author and popular conference speaker. Brenda has conducted countless women conferences and has been invited to speak extensively as a keynote speaker both locally and abroad.

Brenda has served as worship leader, intercessory prayer leader, Sunday school superintendent, counselor, life coach, as well as a host for family life conferences for women retreats, mother-and-daughter branches, and single events.

Brenda recently started her own Podcast called, The Nexxt Chapter where her main focus and expertise will be to pour into the nurturing and cultivating that is designed to meet her audience exactly where they are in life and to provide encouragement as well as motivation that will challenge them to become their own best version of themselves.

Brenda uniquely weaves her life story and her powerful teaching to create a message of encouragement, hope, and motivation to all. A message that challenges everyone to keep their eyes focused on the real prize, and that is none other than Jesus Christ who is Lord over everything.

Also by

Had It Not Been For The Lord On Her Side
ISBN 978-1681188195
(Out of print)

Raw Faith
ISBN 978-0998330822

Forgetting Former Things
ISBN 978-0998330877

Living In Purpose
ISBN 978-1732536333

Cycles
ISBN 978-1732536395

Spiritual Intruders
ISBN 978-1734039856

Necessary Boundaries
ISBN 979-8988648598

The Sunnyside of Heartache

Companion Activities for Personal Growth and Healing

Brenda Murphy

Contents

Fullpage image	188
1. The Sunnyside of Heartache Workbook	189
2. How to Use This Workbook	191
3. Section One: Acknowledging Heartache	192
4. Section Two: Finding the Sunnyside of Your Personal Heartache	194
5. Section Three: Moving Forward Through Your Private Pain	196
6. Section Four: The Importance of Self-Care in Your Heartache	198
7. Section Five: Making Your Personal a Priority in Your Healing	200
8. Section Six: Setting New Boundaries for the Journey Ahead	202
9. Section Seven: Having a New Perspective in The Journey Ahead:	204
10. Section Eight: Trusting God With Your Future	206

11. Section Nine: Finding Rest in God While Processing Your Personal Pain — 208

12. Section Ten: Trusting God With Your Future: — 210

13. Section Eleven: It Greater Later: — 212

14. Section Twelve: How Important is it to be Patient With Your New Chapter? — 214

15. Section Thirteen: Finding Rest in God While Processing Personal Pain — 216

16. Section Fourteen: Setting The Stage For Future Success — 218

17. Conclusion — 220

18. Embracing God's Timing for Your Life — 224

19. Notes & Reflections — 226

20. Closing Thoughts — 232

21. Closing Prayer for Healing from Heartache — 243

About the author — 245

Also by Brenda Murphy — 247

The Sunny Side of Heartache Workbook

Isaiah 40:31(NIV)

"But those who hope in the Lord will renew their strength. They will soar on wings like eagles; they will run and not grow weary; they will walk and not be faint."

Isaiah 40:31

Chapter One

The Sunnyside of Heartache Workbook

Companion Activities for Personal Growth and Healing

Welcome to ***The Sunnyside of Heartache Workbook***. This companion guide is designed to help you reflect, process, and grow as you journey through the themes of your book. Each section includes thoughtful prompts, exercises, and space for your own insights, supporting you in finding hope and resilience amidst life's challenges.

Chapter Two

How to Use This Workbook

- Read each chapter of *The Sunnyside of Heartache* and then complete the corresponding section in this workbook.

- Take your time with each activity—these exercises are meant for honest reflection.

- Write directly in the spaces provided or use a separate journal if you prefer.

- Revisit activities as you continue your healing journey.

Acknowledging our personal heartache is a crucial step in the healing process. The Bible provides numerous verses that emphasize the importance of recognizing and validating our personal pain. Below are some key scriptures that highlight this aspect:

Psalm 34:18 (NIV): "The Lord is close to the brokenhearted and saves those who are crushed in spirit."

Romans 8:28 (NIV): "And we know that in all things God works for the good of those who love him, who have been called according to his purpose.."

Matthew 5:4 (ESV): "Blessed are those who mourn, for they shall be comforted."

Chapter Three

Section One: Acknowledging Heartache

1. Reflect: Describe a recent experience of heartache. What were your initial emotions and thoughts?

_____
_____
_____
_____
_____
_____
_____
_____
_____
_____
_____
_____
_____
_____
_____
_____
_____
_____
_____
_____

2. Exercise: List three lessons this experience has taught you about yourself or others.

_____
_____
_____
_____
_____
_____
_____
_____
_____
_____
_____
_____
_____
_____
_____
_____
_____
_____
_____
_____
_____
_____

Philippians 4:13 (ESV): "I can do all things through him who strengthens.

This verse reminds us that God is always with us, even in our darkest moments, and that acknowledging our pain is an important part of our healing journey. By recognizing our heartache, we can draw closer to God, who sees our struggles and understands what we are going through.

Chapter Four

Section Two: Finding the Sunnyside of Your Personal Heartache

1. Prompt: Write about a time when you found hope or positivity after a difficult event. What helped you shift your perspective?

_____
_____
_____
_____
_____
_____
_____
_____
_____
_____
_____
_____
_____
_____
_____
_____
_____
_____
_____
_____

2. Gratitude Exercise: List five things you're grateful for, even in the midst of heartache.

Chapter Five

Section Three: Moving Forward Through Your Private Pain

1. Action Plan: List three small steps you can take this week to nurture yourself.

_____
_____
_____
_____
_____
_____
_____
_____
_____
_____
_____
_____
_____
_____
_____
_____
_____
_____
_____
_____

2. Affirmation: Write a positive affirmation you can repeat to yourself when you're feeling low.

Chapter Six

Section Four: The Importance of Self-Care in Your Heartache

1. Action Plan: List five specific needs to prioritize your self-care and emotional healing.

_____
_____
_____
_____
_____
_____
_____
_____
_____
_____
_____
_____
_____
_____
_____
_____
_____
_____
_____
_____
_____

2. Affirmation: Write a positive affirmation you can do to provide for yourself during self-care while processing heartache.

Chapter Seven

Section Five: Making Your Personal a Priority in Your Healing

1. Make a list of what steps you will take to encourage your move to personalize your healing during your new normal.

_____
_____
_____
_____
_____
_____
_____
_____
_____
_____
_____
_____
_____
_____
_____
_____
_____
_____
_____
_____

2. List five ways that you give yourself space to heal.

Chapter Eight

Section Six: Setting New Boundaries for the Journey Ahead

1. Name ways you plan to set new boundaries for the next chapter in your life.

_____
_____
_____
_____
_____
_____
_____
_____
_____
_____
_____
_____
_____
_____
_____
_____
_____
_____
_____
_____

2. What steps will you use to do so?

Chapter Nine

Section Seven: Having a New Perspective in The Journey Ahead:

1. Name at least five different ways you plan to change the narrative of your perspective in your personal journey ahead.

_____
_____
_____
_____
_____
_____
_____
_____
_____
_____
_____
_____
_____
_____
_____
_____
_____
_____
_____
_____

2. What does this perspective look like in real time?

Chapter Ten

Section Eight: Trusting God With Your Future

1. How willing are you to trust God with your future?

_____
_____
_____
_____
_____
_____
_____
_____
_____
_____
_____
_____
_____
_____
_____
_____
_____
_____
_____

2. Trusting God with our future is crucial. Trusting God with your future involves recognizing His sovereignty, seeking His guidance, and embracing faith through prayer and scripture. How can you apply this scripture to your heartache?

_____
_____
_____
_____
_____
_____
_____
_____
_____
_____
_____
_____
_____
_____
_____
_____
_____
_____
_____
_____
_____
_____
_____
_____
_____
_____
_____

Chapter Eleven

Section Nine: Finding Rest in God While Processing Your Personal Pain

1. Finding rest in the Word of God is vital. Seeking spiritual rest is paramount. Surrendering to God's lordship and dwelling in His presence is important. This involves being still and waiting patiently for God's guidance and peace.

2. Make a list of the necessary steps you will take toward finding rest in God's Word for your personal journey.

Chapter Twelve

Section Ten: Trusting God With Your Future:

1. Proverbs 3:5-6 (NLT) says, "Trust in the Lord with all your heart and lean not on your own understanding; in all your ways submit to him, and he will make your paths straight." How would you apply this scripture to your new journey?

_____
_____
_____
_____
_____
_____
_____
_____
_____
_____
_____
_____
_____
_____
_____
_____
_____
_____
_____
_____

2. What does that trust look like for you, especially in our culture today?

Chapter Thirteen

Section Eleven: It Greater Later:

1. Trusting God means embracing His timing. Ecclesiastes 3:1 (NIV) reminds us, "There is a time for everything, and a season for every activity under the heavens." Name several ways that you find waiting on God's timing in your life challenging. What are some ways you can change your thinking?

_____
_____
_____
_____
_____
_____
_____
_____
_____
_____
_____
_____
_____
_____
_____
_____
_____
_____

2. Name some specific things you would like to see come to fruition in your next chapter.

Chapter Fourteen

Section Twelve: How Important is it to be Patient With Your New Chapter?

1. Do you believe God has a blessing with your name on it? If so, how?

_____
_____
_____
_____
_____
_____
_____
_____
_____
_____
_____
_____
_____
_____
_____
_____
_____
_____
_____
_____
_____

2. Talk about what insight may look like to you now?

Chapter Fifteen

Section Thirteen: Finding Rest in God While Processing Personal Pain

1. Name four things you can do today to begin your journey toward finding rest in God while walking through your personal heartache.

2. How important is finding rest through the Word of God to you during your healing process?

Chapter Sixteen

Section Fourteen: Setting The Stage For Future Success

1. Through the Word of God, list several ways you can begin to set the stage for a new lifestyle in your new journey.

_____
_____
_____
_____
_____
_____
_____
_____
_____
_____
_____
_____
_____
_____
_____
_____
_____
_____
_____
_____
_____

2. According to Proverbs 19:21 (NIV), "Many are the plans in a person's heart, but it is the Lord's purpose that prevails." While this verse reassures us that God's plans are greater than our own, it also encourages us to release control and trust His perfect wisdom. List some personal ways you can release total control to God's perfect will for your life.

Chapter Seventeen

Conclusion

Developing a consistent prayer life is crucial. Pray about your day-to-day decisions, big and small, and invite God into every aspect of your life. Philippians 4:6 (ESV) encourages us to "not be anxious about anything, but in everything, by prayer and supplication, with thanksgiving, let your requests be made known to God." This practice helps us build trust and allows God to direct our paths.

Chapter Eighteen

Embracing God's Timing for Your Life

1. Share your personal thoughts for God's timing in your life.

_____
_____
_____
_____
_____
_____
_____
_____
_____
_____
_____
_____
_____
_____
_____
_____
_____
_____
_____
_____
_____
_____
_____

2. What matters most to you with God's timing in your new lifestyle?

Chapter Nineteen

Notes & Reflections

Use this space for additional thoughts, memories, or insights you experience while working through the book.

_____
_____
_____
_____
_____
_____
_____
_____
_____
_____
_____
_____
_____
_____
_____
_____
_____
_____
_____
_____

Chapter Twenty

Closing Thoughts

Remember, heartache is a universal experience, but so is resilience. Give yourself grace as you heal and grow and let this workbook be a gentle companion on your journey to a sunnier tomorrow.

Chapter Twenty-One

Closing Prayer for Healing from Heartache

Heavenly Father,

In this quiet moment, I lay my pain before You. You see the tears I've hidden, the weight I've carried, and the wounds I cannot put into words. Wrap me in Your unfailing love and remind me that even in my brokenness, I am never alone. Give me the strength to release what I cannot change, the courage to face each new day, and the hope to believe that joy will return. Heal the places in my heart that feel empty and fill them with Your peace that surpasses all understanding.

Thank You for being my refuge, my comfort, and my guide. I trust that You are turning this pain into purpose, and that in Your perfect time, You will restore my joy.

In Jesus' Name, Amen.

About the author

BRENDA MURPHY is a captivating and inspirational Christian author and popular conference speaker. Brenda has conducted countless women conferences and has been invited to speak extensively as a keynote speaker both locally and abroad.

Brenda has served as worship leader, intercessory prayer leader, Sunday school superintendent, counselor, life coach, as well as a host for family life conferences for women retreats, mother-and-daughter branches, and single events.

Brenda recently started her own Podcast called, The Nexxt Chapter where her main focus and expertise will be to pour into the nurturing and cultivating that is designed to meet her audience exactly where they are in life and to provide encouragement as well as motivation that will challenge them to become their own best version of themselves.

Brenda uniquely weaves her life story and her powerful teaching to create a message of encouragement, hope, and motivation to all. A message that challenges everyone to keep their eyes focused on the real prize, and that is none other than Jesus Christ who is Lord over everything.

Also by Brenda Murphy

Had It Not Been For The Lord On Her Side
ISBN 978-1681188195
(Out of print)

Raw Faith
ISBN 978-0998330822

Forgetting Former Things
ISBN 978-0998330877

Living In Purpose
ISBN 978-1732536333

Cycles
ISBN 978-1732536395

Spiritual Intruders
ISBN 978-1734039856

Necessary Boundaries
ISBN 979-8988648598

www.ingramcontent.com/pod-product-compliance
Lightning Source LLC
Chambersburg PA
CBHW070640160426
43194CB00009B/1523